Haunted Liverpool 22

Tom Slemen

Copyright © 2013 Tom Slemen

All rights reserved.

ISBN-10: 1489568573
ISBN-13: **978-1489568571**

DEDICATION

For my grandmother Rose Slemen

CONTENTS

Introduction	1
An Invisible Assailant in Menlove Gardens	18
Exactly Like You	26
Nobody	32
Close Encounters with Angels	37
A Curious Cavern Ghost	41
Another Abduction at St Luke's	44
Stalked by Death	49
The Men in Black	56
Who Haunted Whom?	64
Dreams of Murder	67
Mysteries of the Space-Time Continuum	73
When Jesus Calls	82
William	86
Mammon	92
The Mad Widow	97

Halewood's Old Hag	101
In a Vision Once I Saw	107
The Sinister	118
A Warning Voice from Beyond	126
The Pact	137
Edge Lane Hall	141
Mary	147
The Grinning Man Scare	151
An Aigburth Zombie?	156
Haunting Melodies	159
Some Violent Liverpool Ghosts	162
The Dabblers	172
Long Arms	180
A Norris Green Haunting	183
Mr Holt	194
Night Nurse Tales	197
Some Headless Ghosts	202

The Vanished	209
A Pair of Blue Eyes	222
St Mark's Eve	232
The Ghost of a Murderer	242
In the Twinkling of an Eye	246
Henry	253
Truth Be Told	258
Unrequited	262
A Strange Force of Attraction	266
The Delhi Eye	274
A Night with a Dead Man	278
There's Always Someone Watching	288

INTRODUCTION

People often ask me: 'Where do you get your stories from?' and the answer to this question is straightforward; I look for some stories by scouring old books in libraries and by scanning many miles of old newspapers in the same libraries, and occasionally I am given access to private collections of out-of-print books and Victorian and Edwardian diaries which will provide me with some beautiful gem of a tale. The other source is the public. Everywhere I go, people have a tale to tell, even the sceptics who tell me there are no ghosts or that the supernatural is all in the mind – they usually then add, 'Mind you, one strange thing did happen to me once,' and then they will tell me a story about a ghost, or a UFO sighting, or some inexplicable time loss, or apparent reincarnation, or of a warning in a dream and so on. I recall one taxi driver picking me up to take me to a certain radio station where I was to talk about the paranormal, and this driver, speaking to me via his rear-view mirror (as many cabbies do) said he found the whole idea of ghosts hard to believe – and then he said, 'Mind you, there was one weird incident years ago, when I was involved in a crash. I had just been in a collision with a car near Picton Road, Wavertree – and this was about – let me see now – about seven years ago. Anyway after the collision I got out to have a look at the damage to my cab, and got hit by a passing car. Hit and run it was. Car just slammed into me, right? I was gone, black out with the shock, right?'

'Go on,' I replied to his eyes in the rear view mirror. I was intrigued.

'Now this is on my kid's life, no word of a lie, Tom,' he assured me, and I noticed him touch a Holy Rosary dangling from the dashboard. 'I came around and the ambulance and police hadn't arrived yet, and I was on my back in the road, thinking, I'm either dying or am going to be okay, but I could hardly move like. Anyway, I noticed a few people standing over me – this is just by the railway bridge which goes over Picton Road – and I'm thinking, and hoping, that these bystanders have phoned for an ambulance – and then I saw this fellah – white suit, long hair, old style wire-framed National Health specs on – and I suddenly realised who it was: John Lennon.'

'Lennon?' I am now really intrigued.

'John Lennon Tom, on my kid's life. He looked like he did around the time of Abbey Road, you know, where you seem him walking over the zebra crossing with the other Beatles in his white suit. So anyway, I'm laying there, looking up at him, and I could hardly speak, and I said: "Lennon?" and he smiled, and he said: "Strange days indeed," and It wasn't just someone who looked like him – it was him, you know his voice? We've heard it that much – it wasn't just someone putting it on. Now, he said something else to me and it was something reassuring me I'd be okay and that help was on the way, but I must have conked out around then because I can't remember what he said.'

'So you saw a ghost, even though you don't believe in them?' I asked.

The cabby was silent for a while, then said: 'I suppose so in a way. What do you think he's been? I didn't imagine it. I mean, I'm not even into the Beatles, never have been, more into Pink Floyd and Fleetwood Mac – so why did he appear to me?'

I told the cabby Lennon's ghost had allegedly been seen across Liverpool, as well as certain parts of New York. The hotspots for the sightings were the murdered Beatles' former home – "Mendips", at 251 Menlove Avenue, and Strawberry Field on Beaconsfield Road, just around the corner from Mendips. I told the cabby how I was researching sightings of what are believed to be ghostly orphans from the former Strawberry Field orphanage a few years back when I saw a man who looked exactly like the figure that had appeared to him – and I believed at the time it was just some Beatles fanatic visiting the iconic red gates of Strawberry Field dressed up as Lennon, but then this man in the snow-white suit and long hair vanished, along with an old woman (believed to have been John's beloved Aunt Mimi). When Sir Paul McCartney did a concert in Liverpool's King's Dock, many years ago, I had scores of reports of Lennon's ghost being seen near the waterfront venue as well as other locations. I naturally assumed it was just someone purposely dressing up as Lennon in his trademark white suit and wire-frame glasses, but I even had a detailed report from a policeman who saw a man the image of Lennon vanish before his eyes on Sefton Street (the dock road). There were also reports of the same figure being seen near Gambier Terrace, off Hope Street, in the shadow of the Anglican Cathedral, and funnily enough, Lennon once lived at Gambier Terrace with Stuart Sutcliffe, a former Beatles bassist who tragically died from a brain haemorrhage in 1962, just before the Fab Four became world famous. Sutcliffe was buried in Huyton Parish Church Cemetery, but the ghost of this Lost Beatle has allegedly been seen around Gambier Terrace – where he once shared a room with Lennon in their Bohemian days. In July 1989, scores of people attending a Julian Lennon concert at the Royal Court claimed that Lennon's ghost appeared onstage halfway through Julian's set of songs paying homage to his father, and some of those who saw the alleged solid-looking phantom said they had seen the same figure during a vigil on Mathew Street nine years before when Lennon had been assassinated.

A distinguished-looking gentleman who bore a strong resemblance to the late actor Jon Pertwee (of Doctor Who and Worzel Gummidge fame) once came up to my table during a booksigning at

Waterstones and told me he wanted two books signed for his children, who were avid fans of my work. This man then mentioned in passing that he didn't believe in ghosts – 'But,' he then added, 'the hospital I work in is haunted; I wonder if you know anything about it?'

It transpired that the silver-haired semi-sceptic was a surgeon at the hospital concerned, and he told me: 'A few weeks back a nursing sister and a couple of the nurses under her saw some amorphous, shapeless thing at the end of the ward, about two in the morning. One of the nurses said she didn't believe in ghosts and decided to see what this thing was, but when she walked up to it she couldn't get past it, and she later said it was like trying to get past an invisible brick wall. The nursing sister tried to get past this obstruction as well, and found it impossible, and all three nurses had to turn around and go through a door that took them down several corridors to get to the doorway leading to the other end of the ward. They said there was a vague smoky outline of a woman standing there. The nursing sister asked this thing why it was haunting the ward, and a voice – a soft female voice – answered, saying it wanted to look after the patients. It then vanished. We have been told that a staff sister died on this haunted ward about twenty years back and she had been seen standing at the bedsides of patients.'

'And do you doubt the testimony of the nurses?' I asked.

The surgeon smiled and said, 'I'm not doubting them, but I just find it hard to believe. So many people unfortunately die in hospitals, so the places would be overrun with spirits, but that's what I was told anyway. Have you heard about the ghost in that hospital?'

I told him I was familiar with the hauntings there, and not only supplied the surgeon with the name of the staff sister who is believed to be haunting the ward, I also related many stories of the hospital he was not aware of, and then, as people became impatient in the long queue behind the surgeon, he quickly told me how, on one occasion as he carried out a life or death operation, he had seen the exact double of the man he was operating on floating about in the operating theatre. I duly jotted this account down for future use. Considering the surgeon's alleged disbelief in ghosts, he told me some interesting tales.

A ferret-faced man in his forties approached me once at Churchill's, a club that used to stand on leafy Church Road , Wavertree where I put on many well-attended talks about local ghosts. I had just finished my last story about a local haunting and was sitting down, sipping bitter shandy when this gentleman came up to me and told me he loved the stories, but was still an agnostic – he neither believed or disbelieved – 'But,' he went on, 'years ago when I was in my teens I was always in trouble with the law; I've changed since those days thank God, but I think I might have ended up murdering someone if I hadn't seen the light, but that's another story. Anyway, this was when I was eighteen. I had broken into a well-known store in the city centre and made off with quite a few bob in my tail, an then, someone grassed on me. The police turned up at our house this night, which, I will never forget, was one of the foggiest nights ever, and when my dad asked who was calling they shouted "Police!" and then one of them started kicking the door in as my 'arl fellah was trying to get the bolt off. I panicked, ran into the backyard, thinking I'd escape, and there were two coppers waiting outside in the entry. I climbed onto the backyard wall and ran along it – and this is in a thick fog – and I ran and ran, and I thought I'd lose my footing because as you can imagine Tom, a brick wall in an entry is about a foot wide if it's that. I could hear the copper running after me down the entry and one of them fell over some bin bags and then I leaped right across this jigger and almost broke my neck. I landed on another wall to a back yard and then scrambled onto this slanting roof and next thing I was up on a roof. I almost slipped as a few slates came loose and then I remember being perched up against a chimney stack and when I looked down, all I could see was fog and a few of the lamp post lights just about showing through. I remember seeing blue flashes from the bizzies' cars, and my heart was in my mouth. I then got on my hands and knees and got across this roof and thought I'd put as much distance as I could between me and the law. I ended up dropping onto the roof of what I thought was a garage for some reason, and I tried a narrow window, and it actually opened with the loudest squeak ever. I almost died getting through this window at a real awkward angle, because I went in feet first and then I sort of felt the frame digging into my back, and I was hanging backwards from my waist out the window, and I thought I'd either break my spine in two or I'd slip out and fall head-first into the yard. I was swearing and everything, and then I somehow managed to slide into the window, and knocked my chin badly as I did, but at least I was now inside what I thought was a garage. I looked around inside and didn't dare turn the light on for obvious reasons, and I hoped and prayed the place didn't have any alarms. My stupid plan was to lay low in this place and then go to a friend's house and then try and live abroad in France. I was a dickhead in those days. I went down some stairs to have a nose about and went along a hallway into a large windowless room where I decided I'd switch a light on, as no one would see anything outside because there were no windows, like. It was a butcher's refrigeration room, and I could see the big cream-coloured drawers and heavy enamelled doors where the meat was hung up. I then left this room and went into a carpeted room which smelt of lavender or roses, and I couldn't switch a light on in here, but I kept flicking on my lighter as I looked about. Then I heard voices. It sounded like two women gabbing away. They sounded nearby but I couldn't find out exactly where they were. I sat on an old upright chair – it looked like a dining chair, and my back was killing me from where I had scraped it against the window frame getting into the place. I just felt like some lemmo or a cup of tea, I was parched. Anyway, in the doorway to my right, which had light shining through it from the refrigeration room, I saw two shadows. Someone was coming this way. I nearly crapped. I saw the heads and shoulders of the long shadows coming along the carpet from the doorway, and heard the voices of the women clearly now. One was saying "I can't get used to it can you?" and the other one was saying "No, I can't," and I actually tried to hide behind this old dining chair. I looked up from behind the back of the chair and saw in the semi-darkness that the two women were dressed in white robes of some sort. One was about five seven and had a big head of curly black hair and she must have been in her early thirties, and the other one was about five three, bit fat, and had greyish or blonde hair to her shoulders, and she looked about late forties early fifties. If they had seen me, and I expected them to see me, I would have just ran out the room and tried to get out of what I assumed was a butcher's shop. But one minute the women were there, and then the next minute they were gone. I wondered where they had gone to so fast, and looked about. I wondered if someone else would come through the doorway, and waited for ages, crouching behind the chair. And then all of a sudden I thought I saw something like two greyish smudges of light leave the room I was hiding in and go back through that doorway. It seemed like a very long time as I waited there, and eventually I thought frig it, and I went into the doorway and saw and heard nothing. I decided it was time to move on, but being a thief, I had to open the meat drawers, and when I did I got the shock of my life. There was a dead woman in the first one – and this was to be the only drawer I ever opened. It was that woman I had seen earlier, only her hair was covered with what looked like a white balaclava, and she was wrapped in a burial shroud. My stomach turned and I felt my heart jumping in my chest. I had broken into a chapel of rest, and realised later where this was. It was a chapel of rest annexed to a funeral director's building. I slammed that drawer shut and ran blindly back the way I had come, but couldn't get back out through that narrow window. I had to go back downstairs and look about until I found a backyard door with a simple Yale lock, and I turned it and ran through the yard and climbed the wall. I got about half a mile away, and as I was walking down a main road, I heard a car's tyres softly moving steadily to my right. I knew who it was. A torchbeam came on and shone in my face and a voice said, "Come on lad!" And I went to the police car. I already had two convictions for burglary but I was glad to be back with the living, but I never admitted 'accidentally' breaking into the chapel of rest.'

It was quite a story from a self-confessed agnostic, and I told the now-reformed and much older gentleman how that chapel of rest had many other strange stories attached to it. A man named Doug was lying in his coffin in that chapel so people could pay their last respects before he was buried for eternity, and yet scores of people saw him on the eve of his funeral, sitting in a quiet corner of his favourite pub, which lay just thirty yards from the funeral parlour. When someone approached the ghost of Doug and asked him how he had returned, he smiled and faded away into the smoky atmosphere of the pub.

So, these are just a few of the ways that stories come in my direction, and they are from the so-called disbelievers. Many more come from people who know that ghosts and timewarps and other strange phenomena exist, and over the years I have come to overlook one important factor in the circumstances of my personal quest to explore the supernatural, and it is this: we are living in a magical land. The Ancient Phoenicians called Britain the Hyperborean Isles, a mysterious land on the northern fringes of the known world enshrouded in mists, peopled with magical wizards (Druids), and criss-crossed with enigmatic lines of ominous power which linked temples, artificial mounds and all sizes of standing stone which dot the varied landscape. I know from personal investigations lasting many years that there are ancient forces sleeping in the earth of my homeland that are probably better left dormant, and I am not just talking about one specific area of the British Isles, but our region – Lancashire and the artificially constructed "Merseyside" area, as well as Cheshire and Wirral. There is a whole corpus of hidden knowledge lying there in our landscape, just waiting to be read by those who can tune into the ancient mind; geodetic forces that dowsers often detect are but a small percentage of the energies we know virtually nothing of, and they are part of this unseen world which exists all around us. Races that have long vanished knew about this other side of nature, but their knowledge seems to have been lost in the Dark Ages, when the Celts went into decline, and by the time the Romans had left Britain, this ancient wisdom was known only to a handful of initiates. There was once a race that was neither Saxon or Briton, and these people – now thought to be extinct - had long skulls – technically known as dolichocephalic – and they were also dark-skinned. These mysterious black people were once thought to have been Saracens brought back to England by the Crusaders, but this is now known to be false, for these puzzling folk were already a part of this island nation long before the Romans arrived here, and possibly predate the Celts too. Ley lines and megaliths are not the only things which cover our land – various representations of the Zodiac have also been traced and carved into our landscape, the most well known of these being the one at Glastonbury, which was rediscovered in modern times (in 1929) by Kathleen Maltwood, an artist and scholarly 'sensitive' who found the Zodiac whilst poring over large scale Ordnance Survey maps. There are many other alleged zodiacal figures now evident which came to light with aerial photography, and we even have one in the North West – the Wirral Zodiac, one of our best kept local secrets. If you know where to look, you may see this ancient astrological pantheon set out in a vast gargantuan circle. Our original Zodiac incidentally, had not twelve, but thirteen signs. The Babylonian one had eighteen signs, the Aztec Zodiac had twenty, and the Ancient Egyptian Zodiac had thirty-six, whereas the Chinese had but four signs of the Zodiac. On three separate continents, archaeologists have found ancient tablets and stones depicting a thirteen-sign Zodiac. The finds were made on

Depuch Island, Australia (on an Aboriginal stone), and on a stone near Hot Springs, Arkansas, and in Greece (a tablet inscribed by thirteen signs, used by the Pelasgian Greeks),but what happened to these forms of the Zodiac and what was the thirteenth sign? Well, if you were born between 13 May and June 10, you are born under the sign of Arachne – the Spider – and the zodiacal symbol of this lost sign is a circle with four spokes in the centre (like the cross-hairs of a gun-sight). Two thousand years ago, when Imperial Rome became a seat of church authority, the Christians eradicated all of the old religions and cults – because it saw them as rivals – and the Thirteenth Sign of the Zodiac was also suppressed because it had very strong associations with the Occult and the ancient cult of Moon-worship. Perhaps it is time to reinstate this lost sign of the Zodiac.

This book also touches on the subject of timeslips, as many of the *Haunted Liverpool* books do. Mark my words, it may sound like bad science fiction, but the Time Race is now on, and the military scientists of most countries are striving to build working time machines, because the person who can move through time can destroy his enemy before he was born and control the course of history. Once upon a time we had the Space Race, when Russia and America were trying their utmost to be the first into space, and the first to land a human on the Moon. The Russians got the first man into space – Yuri Gagarin in April 1961 – and that momentous achievement shamed America and spurred them on to put the first man – the late Neil

Armstrong – onto the face of the Moon in July 1969. Now it is the Time Race, and the militarization of time has always been one of my biggest fears, because it would perhaps be easy to go back and help Hitler win WWII, or to go back further into time and assassinate William the Conqueror so the time travelling army can meddle with the politics of eleventh century England. At the moment, teleportation – the transporting of physical objects across space via beams of light and other electromagnetic waves – is in its infancy, but progress has been made, with scientists teleporting photons and atoms across a room. The next obvious step is to teleport a molecule – and then a virus – and what can be teleported across space can probably be teleported through time, and this would mean that future terrorists could cause epidemics by sending some of the deadliest viruses years, decades or centuries into the past to kill their unsuspecting victims and change history in the process. For hundreds of years, some strange things have been found deep in the earth, in layers belonging to the days of the dinosaurs. A 500 million-year-old hammer was found partially embedded in rock in the 1930s by a Mr and Mrs Hahn when they were out walking in Texas. The hammer, made of about 96% iron, was partly encased in material thought to be at least from the pre-Quaternary stratum - which made it millions of years old – long before modern man had appeared on earth. Other, equally baffling "anomalous fossils" have been excavated which seem to prove that the evolutionists are either completely wrong, and that man is millions of years

older than previously though..
time-travellers have left various ar..
visits to the remote past. Of course, ex..
may be to blame for these out-of-place foss..
can't imagine a star-traveller using a woo..
handled hammer of the kind found by Mr and M..
Hahn. Footprints of human beings have been found in sandstone laid down 225 and 280 million years ago (in the Carboniferous period) – 250 millions before men and apes went their separate way on the evolutionary tree, according to the Darwinists. In 1851, a miner who had dug up a block of auriferous quartz accidentally dropped it, and was surprised to find a straight iron nail embedded in the centre of this block, meaning that nail was manufactured millions of years ago – but by whom? In 1829, a block of marble excavated from a quarry in Philadelphia split perfectly with the chisels of expert stonemasons to expose a strange indentation with two letters of an unknown language visible in it. Chains and coins of an unknown denomination have also been found in such ancient rocks and these objects are a real headache to the archaeologist, the palaeontologist and the evolutionist, for they are almost impossible to explain. We have to opt for remote civilizations which have long vanished from this world and left only the vestiges of their achievements behind – or, we have to consider the possibility that time-travellers have left the objects behind on trips into prehistory. Maybe some of these trips were just exploratory ones, but perhaps some of these journeys across the millennia were missions with

d history. Come to unable to explain just dinosaurs — apparently million years ago. It was the world would ever see. Every from the ones that lived in deserts ed creatures in snow-covered parts wiped out, as well as many species of mammals, shellfish and plants. A plague was suspected at first, but what type of plague could spread almost at lighting speed and even kill plankton and ammonites in the oceans too? A supernova is a more realistic possibility. When a star runs out of its nuclear fuel it swells and collapses in on itself and explodes with a cataclysmic ferocity and showers planets with an emission of deadly radiation for light years around. Such a star, exploding at even a distance of 100 light years, in the days of the dinosaurs, would cause catastrophic changes by blasting the upper protective regions of the atmosphere and ozone layer, as well as showering all life with lethal cosmic rays. The littler creatures, such as shrews and lizards would possibly be able to burrow deep underground and escape the effects of the radiation storm and hibernate until it was safe to surface. These survivors of the exploding star would then, according to the theory of evolution, evolve into the ancestors of man. The dinosaurs departed from this earth in one of the biggest bangs since the one that allegedly started this universe, and with their death, the scene was set for man to take over the planet. Was this just down to an exploding sun, or — well, sometimes I wonder if time-travellers with a neutron bomb or two could have had something to do with it all…

>Tom Slemen,
>"The Bureau",
>Rodney Street
>Liverpool L1

AN INVISIBLE ASSAILANT IN MENLOVE GARDENS

Around 5pm on Thursday 22 November 2012, a couple in their thirties named Nicola and Sean hailed a cab on Liverpool's Hanover Street. It was a cold wet afternoon and already darkness was falling as the couple climbed into the hackney cab carrying plastic and paper carrier bags from a shopping trip that had taken in Cath Kidston, John Lewis, Primark and many other local stores. Nicola had bought a few more Christmas presents for her family and Sean's, as she was quite organised in that way, whereas Sean had bought himself two pairs of cheap jeans at Primark and a book of guitar chords from Waterstones, as he was trying to teach himself to play the old acoustic Nicola had bought him for his 35th birthday a few months before. The couple lived together off Woolton Road, and Nicola instructed the taxi driver to take her and Sean to this destination, but just a few minutes into the journey,

Nicola tugged on Sean's arm and whispered, 'Can you smell that?' And she screwed up her pretty face because she found the aroma in the cab so sickly.

Sean couldn't smell anything because he'd just got over a cold and was still sniffling, but Nicola described the awful odour to him. 'Smells like milk that's gone off, and baby sick', she said and she covered her mouth with her scarf.

'I'll have to go up Smithdown,' the cabby said, his eyes meeting Sean's in the rear view mirror. 'There's roadworks on Picton Road, see.'

'Yeah, alright mate,' Sean said, relaxing in the cold back seat with shopping bags on his lap, and two on the floor.

'Take them off the floor,' Nicola advised her boyfriend, and her voice was raising itself up from a whisper because she was so annoyed at the thought of sitting in a taxi in which someone had obviously been sick.

'Why?' Sean asked, baffled.

'Someone's been sick on that floor, and they could have been ill with a stomach bug; that's all we need,' Nicola replied, and now she could detect the sharp sweet antiseptic traceries of some disinfectant that the cabby had used to clean up the floor after the person had been sick. Nicola wondered if some drunken passenger who'd had too much to drink had been sick in the cab, or was it perhaps a child who had succumbed to one of those stomach bugs that seem to do the rounds in the schools of Liverpool once the autumn slides into winter. She pressed the switch on the taxi door and the window wound down to let in a rush of cold air that buffeted her long eyelashes. Sean suddenly did the same. He said he could now smell the dreadful stench as well, which was unusual for him, not only because he was recovering from a head cold and the continually dripping nose, he never had much of a sense of smell anyway, and rarely knew when Nicola was wearing her expensive scents whenever they were out.

'I'm going to have to tell him to pull over here or I'm going to be sick,' Nicola told her boyfriend, and the scarf covering her lips moved as she spoke. 'Just here'll do mate!' she shouted, and the cabby pulled over at the corner of Menlove Avenue and Menlove Gardens West. Sean gave him a tenner and told him to keep the £1.20 change, and then he and Nicola walked up the gloomy tree-lined road. The pavements of Menlove Gardens West were slicked with wet decomposing leaves. As Sean passed Number 25 Menlove Gardens West, he smiled and looked at the door of the house there, and Nicola rolled her eyes and said, 'Don't say it.'

But Sean did. He said 'I wonder if Qualtrough's home?'

Sean was something of a true crime reader, and he was referring to the alibi of William Herbert Wallace, an insurance salesman who was lured out of his house in Anfield one January evening in 1931 by a man who gave the name R. M. Qualtrough. Qualtrough posed as a potential client, wanting to discuss an insurance policy regarding his daughter, and he requested Mr Wallace to call at his house, at 25 Menlove Gardens East on the very night that Wallace's frail old wife was brutally battered to death by an unknown murderer – who was presumably Qualtrough. Wallace went in search for Qualtrough that night and discovered that there was no Menlove Gardens East – only a Menlove Gardens North, South and West, and so he called at 25 Menlove Gardens West, but no one at that address knew anyone named Qualtrough, and when Wallace returned home, he found that someone had battered his wife's brains out. The full facts of this case can be found in my book, *Murders of Merseyside*. Sean had read a lot about the classic unsolved murder over the years, and so, whenever he and his girlfriend passed 25 Menlove Gardens West, Sean would always make the boring remark about Qualtrough.

On this occasion the couple crossed over the road, away from 25 Menlove Gardens West, and when they were about ten yards from the junction of Dudlow Lane, Sean heard an almighty crack, and Nicola screamed, dropped her shopping bags, and grabbed her left leg, just above the knee. At this point, Sean saw a long branch, about two-and-a-half feet in length, floating in the air to the left of his girlfriend. Nicola was in absolute agony because, she said, something had just whipped her. Within seconds, the branch flew across the road and into the shadows, beyond the feeble amber illumination of the weak sodium vapour street lamp.

Nicola swore and said a branch must have fallen onto her leg, and yet there was no such tree near enough, and this branch had really whacked her as if – well as if someone had been holding the other end of it. Knowing Nicola was terrified of ghosts, Sean waited until they got into the hallway of their flat, when he told her what he'd witnessed. Nicola didn't take it in at first, and when she took off her jeans, she was amazed to see a long red line running along her leg, about five inches up from her kneecap. 'Oh my God it's left a welt, see?' she said, pointing at the six-inch-long red raised line in her flesh.

'I saw the branch that did that float away in mid-air,' Sean said, and his eyes met Nicola's and she knew when he was lying, and she could tell straight away he was telling the truth This strange little incident naturally spooked the couple, and they now refuse to walk anywhere near Menlove Gardens West after dark. Nicola emailed me with her account of this strange occurrence, and I immediately went to my Mossley Hill files and knew exactly where to look, because I had long known about the so-called "Invisible Man" – a mysterious unseen presence that had inflicted so many injuries over the years. Here's a potted history of this entity. A woman named Ruth Campbell was a 14-year-old girl in the 1950s, and in the summer months during the school holidays she enjoyed playing tennis, especially at the tennis courts that existed in the vast triangle of green in the centre of Menlove Gardens North, South and West in Mossley Hill. On one occasion, Ruth and her friend played tennis until dusk was falling, and around 10pm, her opponent – another 14-year-old girl named Susan – suggested they should call it a day. 'Oh let's just play one more game,' Ruth was saying, when suddenly, Susan appeared to jump backwards about four feet, as if she had tried to do an unsuccessful back-flip. The girl landed on her back with a thump, still clutching her tennis racket – and then after a pause, the girl began to cry as blood dripped steadily from her nose and ran down her cheeks and chin in rivulets. 'Susan!' Ruth screamed, and went to her friend's aid. Susan got up and began to run towards Menlove Avenue, sobbing and talking insensibly as Ruth tried to ask her what had happened. An elderly man produced a handkerchief and went to Susan and calmed her down. He told her to hold her head back as he gently pinched her nose. He dabbed the blood on her face, and Susan then said someone had belted her in the face. 'It wasn't me,' Ruth assured the man, and the old Samaritan asked Susan who had struck her. 'I don't know,' Susan said, and began to cry again. The elderly man told Ruth to take her friend home immediately and the girls set off for Susan's home on Addingham Road, just a few minutes' walk away. Susan's mother naturally wanted to know who had punched her daughter and Ruth said she had seen no one near her friend; Susan had just been knocked backwards by something. 'That's ridiculous', Susan's mum said, 'you must have seen the person who hit her; you were there, weren't you? Are you and Susan being bullied by someone?'

'I swear I didn't see anyone, and neither did Susan,' Ruth told her friend's mum, and Susan's grandfather suddenly said that he had heard about a ghost that haunted Menlove Gardens a few years back. Susan's mother said ghosts didn't exist and wouldn't go round punching innocent girls if they did, and Ruth had the impression that her friend's grandfather wanted to tell a little more about the ghost, but never got a chance, and Ruth never did find out what the old man knew.

The girls were so affected by the freak incident, they never again went to play tennis in Menlove Gardens.

I received a letter a few years back from a man named Eric who, in 1996, lived on Montclair Drive in Wavertree, and most mornings before work and some evenings after work, he would take his Old English sheepdog Jeeves for long walks, and most of these walks took in Menlove Gardens as well as Calderstones Park on some occasions. One wintry December night in 1996, Eric took Jeeves on a half-hour stroll. The time was around 10.45pm and Eric was well-wrapped up with a sheepskin coat, woollen hat and scarf, and an old pair of driving gloves on his hands. Jeeves dragged him down Montclair Drive, onto Rutherford Road, and across Queen's Drive. Jeeves knew the way by heart and tugged his owner along Menlove Avenue. Eric planned to go as far as Mendips, John Lennon's old house, but then he decided to turn into Menlove Gardens West because sleet began to fall. Jeeves suddenly latched his nose onto the trunk of a tree and began to sniff. He'd obviously smelt something of great interest, and Eric tugged on the animal's leash a few times and said, 'Come on,' but Jeeves stubbornly remained at the tree for about a minute, and during that time, Eric felt someone brush past him – even though he could see no one. He heard footfalls going away from him, as if someone invisible had run past. And then he saw something triggering the porch lights of each house as it progressed up Menlove Gardens South. These porch lights, as most people are aware, switch on when someone approaches their infra-red sensors. This really spooked Eric, and so he dragged Jeeves from the tree and walked up Menlove Gardens West, intending to leave the unusually quiet and dimly-lit area, but as he reached the junction at Dudlow Lane – the unseen runner came upon him again, and this time Jeeves began to bark and jump at something – as if he could sense the invisible presence. Something slapped the dog in its face, and it yelped – and the animal was then hit again – this time with such ferocity, it howled and yanked the leash from Eric's hands as it ran off. Eric ran after the dog, and thought he heard laughter behind him. Jeeves ran across Queen's Drive, heading for home, and was almost hit by a car. Eric was in a right state when he reached his house on Montclair Drive, but thanked God when he saw poor Jeeves cowering behind bushes in the garden.

What's behind the aforementioned incidents? If it's a ghost haunting Menlove Gardens, why is it so violent? Ghosts on the whole, rarely injure anyone, with the exception of poltergeists, and even poltergeist activity is short-lived, but I feel as if there is something more to this entity than – well, I was going to say 'meets the eye' but this thing is beyond the range of human vision. I will have to dig a little deeper into this case, and perhaps go on a regular vigil around Menlove Gardens to ascertain just what is prowling that area, and to find out why it needs to show its presence in such a brutal way.

EXACTLY LIKE YOU

In December 1980 a 24-year-old Kirkby woman named Mandy Houghton broke up with her boyfriend Terry after she caught him kissing her best friend Joan in a local pub called the Peacock. Mandy was devastated by Terry's infidelity, and her boyfriend claimed he had been drunk when he had kissed Joan, and had not been 'carrying on' with her, but Mandy told him to stay away from her, otherwise she'd have a word with her older brother Charlie – an amateur boxer. Mandy seemed to go into a decline after the break-up with Terry, and her best friend Nicky told her she should give Terry another chance – 'After all, he had been palatic drunk,' Nicky reasoned, but Mandy stubbornly refused to give Terry another chance, but she really felt lonely at Christmas while all her other friends went as couples to the local pub. On Boxing Day, Nicky's cousin invited her to a New Year's Eve party over in Huyton, and Nicky went to this party and took Mandy with her. Everything was going well until Terry turned up. It turned out that Terry had been a school friend of the man who had thrown the party, and Mandy felt very uncomfortable with her ex-boyfriend present. She danced with her friends but Terry kept gawping over at her, and when any male came over to chat to Mandy, Terry would look him up and down with an expression of revulsion. Around 11.40pm, Mandy could no longer take the constant scrutiny from her former boyfriend, and being quite intoxicated, she announced she was going home. 'Don't be soft, Mandy,' Nicky told her, 'you're not leaving. It's nearly midnight. We'll get really drunk after twelve and I'll introduce you to this fellah my sister works with; he's the spitting image of Burt Reynolds.'

'No, I want to go home, I feel sick!' Mandy groaned, and she headed into the hallway, unsteady on her heels, but Nicky somehow prevented her friend from leaving the house and took her upstairs, where she sat Mandy down in a an old armchair in a small box room. Mandy dozed off and she heard something odd; downstairs, someone in the party was playing Blondie's *Hanging On the Telephone* and the song was beginning to reverberate as if it was being played in an echo-chamber. Another song was playing at the same time, and it sounded like *Auld*

Lang Syne, and it was growing in intensity as Mandy drifted away into the realms of sleep. She woke some time later to the smell of cigarette smoke. The door to the box room was ajar, and the silouhette of a tall slim man of six foot or more feet stood there in the rectangle of light. His face was mostly masked in shadow because of this yellow light from the landing shining behind him, and also because Mandy's eyes were a bit blurred after her sleep.

'I say, are you alright there dear?' said the man in a rich deep voice, and Mandy saw him lift a cigarette to his mouth and puff on it so a small point of orange light appeared.

'Where's Nicky?' Mandy asked, and slowly got out of the armchair.

The stranger stepped into the room and helped Mandy out of the chair. He had a peculiar aroma about him that reminded Mandy of mothballs. His hands were soft but firm as he took hold of Mandy by her upper arms and dragged her onto the landing, and here, the Kirkby woman could see that the man was dressed in a rather outdated manner – unless it was fancy dress. His short hair was chestnut coloured, centre-parted and slicked back, and he wore a black fork-tailed coat and matching black trousers that were baggy at the top, and they tapered down to a pair of gleaming black shoes. The quaint-looking tall man also wore a white bow-tie, a type of cravat, and this added to his debonair look. He seemed to be in his late thirties, perhaps early forties, and his grey eyes looked deep into Mandy's as he asked: 'It's so uncanny, so extraordinary.'

'What is?' Mandy asked.

The man smiled, blew a perfect circle of smoke into the air, and said: 'Remember that song, *Exactly Like You*? How does it go now?' And he suddenly started to sing a few lines: 'I used to have a perfect sweetheart, not a real one, just a dream... that song! Do you know it? The best part of it goes: I know why I've waited, know why I've been blue, prayed each night for someone, exactly like you. Do you remember it now?'

Mandy had never heard it before, and she looked past the stranger towards the stairs and asked what time it was because it sounded silent downstairs – as if all the partygoers had left.

'It's late,' said the man, and then he gave a little cough, reached for Mandy's hand and said: 'I'm Gordon by the way,' and he lifted the girl's hand and kissed her knuckle, which startled Mandy. 'I'm Mandy,' she replied, pulling her hand away, 'has everyone gone? What time is it?'

At that moment a group of people downstairs began to sing 'Auld Lang Syne', and a champagne cork popped. Glasses clinked, and the sounds of the singers swelled so that Gordon grimaced, grinned and held his hands to his ears with his cigarette between his lips. The singing died down and Mandy thought she heard ship's horns and cheers somewhere in the distance. 'Happy New Year!' someone exclaimed downstairs, and it was not a voice Mandy recognised, but a plummy well-spoken voice.

'Mandy, as I was saying, it's so extraordinary – you look exactly like my fiancée Julia – well, my ex fiancée I should say. Perhaps you are related? Julia

Durban; you're not one of the Durbans are you?'

Gordon was making Mandy very nervous. She had the creepy idea that this man was some ghost, and then she noticed that he had no shadow. Her shadow was on the floor of the landing but Gordon had no such shadow, and she asked him why he had none. 'I haven't a clue – it's so funny isn't it?' he laughed, but his eyes remained serious and gleamed with faint traceries of spite – as if he was mad because she had seen through his 'act'. He then seized Mandy's wrist and said, 'I've prepared a little something for you up there in the loft where you can join me in a new life,' and he dragged Mandy around a corner in a very forceful manner. Mandy cried out for help. 'Be quiet, my dear, no one can hear you now!' Gordon assured her, and he looked up at the hatch in the ceiling. There was a stepladder below it. Dimly visible in the loft, Mandy could see a rope with a noose hanging over a beam. There were heavy thumps on the stairs. Terry came bounding up those stairs, and all of a sudden, Gordon was flitting up the stepladder, his coat tails flying up behind him in the rush. 'You alright?' Terry asked, and Mandy almost fainted and fell into his arms. She pointed to the ceiling hatch and tried to tell Terry what had happened. Terry saw someone lifting the stepladder into the hatchway. 'Who the hell's that?' he asked.

Gordon fell through that hatch, arms at his sides, and a noose about his neck. Mandy screamed as the body bounced once on the rope then kicked its shiny shoes about. The head fell limp sideways, tongue protruding. Terry swore and took Mandy downstairs. When Terry returned to the landing with three guests, the hatch was still open, but when the men bravely inspected the loft, they found it empty. The terrifying haunting had an everlasting effect on Mandy, and she still has nightmares about Gordon. She got back with Terry and they later married and are still wed today.

It's said that around 1930, a man named Gordon committed suicide at the house during a New Year's Eve party after being jilted by his fiancée. I wonder if his bride-to-be looked just like Mandy?

NOBODY

A few years back, during my fortnightly slot talking about the paranormal on BBC Radio Merseyside's Billy Butler Show, I mentioned reports of a ghostly clown that had been seen in Prescot near a place aptly called Tickle Avenue. The clown had allegedly haunted a house on that avenue since the 1960s at least. Around 1965, a 10-year-old girl went into a derelict house on Tickle Avenue with a friend and there, hanging in an alcove in the front room, was a baggy clown costume of red satin with polka dots with frilly white cuffs, together with a pointed hat - which had a pom-pom sewn into its point. As one of the girls touched the eerie clown outfit, it shimmered as if was just a reflected image in some liquid mirror, and then the costume vanished. When I came out of the studio after mentioning this strange incident, a listener named Kathy called the radio station to tell me the following.

In December 1962, Kathy and her husband Mike and their 9-year-old son Brian, moved into a house in a certain part of Liverpool. About a week after settling in, Brian went into his parents' room around 2am and said a man dressed as a clown was in his room. Brian had awakened to see the peculiar-looking clown crawling on all fours at the side of his bed. The figure had put its index finger to its painted mouth, gesturing for Brian to be quiet, but the boy ran screaming out the room. Brian's father Mike went to the room and found his lad's mattress overturned, and he also smelt something hanging in the air that reminded him of fairground candyfloss after it had just been freshly spun. Mike searched the room and the rest of the house and found no intruders lurking anywhere. 'You've had a nightmare, Brian,' Kathy told her son, but he picked up his school Bible, and placing his hand on it, solemnly swore he had seen a clown in his room. Weeks later, around 8pm on New Year's Eve, Kathy was watching her favourite telly programme, *Harpers West One* when she heard faint male laughter upstairs. Her husband and son were next door helping neighbours to prepare for a Hogmanay party, so Kathy was naturally perplexed and understandably nervous at the sounds she had heard, being alone in the house. But curiosity got the better of her, and so she crept up the stairs towards the source of the laughter – the bathroom. Kathy slowly turned the door handle and peeped in. She got the shock of her life. A man was kneeling over the bath, and was dressed as a clown in a red and black striped outfit, a frilly white ruffled collar, and the hair on either side of his painted bald head was styled into what looked like wings. A green lightning bolt was also painted from the top of his pate to the tomato-sized red nose he wore. 'I'm Nobody the Clown!' he told Kathy, and said something else that she could not make out, and then she saw that he had a carving knife in his gloved hand, and he held this to his throat. As Kathy turned in what felt like slow motion to get away, she heard liquid fall and patter into the bath, and she had the impression that this was the blood falling from a self-inflicted wound in the throat of the clown. She also heard a horrible gurgling sound as she hurried across the landing towards the stairs. In mute terror, Kathy ran out of the house and went to the neighbours to tell her husband what she had just seen, and began to cry. Mike and two men went into the house and found no one at large, but enough was enough, and the family decided to stay with relatives. Kathy's former neighbours later told her that the ghostly clown had been seen at the house for years, and was believed to be the apparition of a clown called Nobody who committed suicide – by cutting his throat as he knelt over the bath. The ghost had seemingly stopped haunting the house for a few years, but had evidently returned with a vengeance.

I mentioned this story on the radio, and was inundated with stories about the same house, even though I had not even mentioned its address. Most of the calls named the road in Liverpool where the haunted house stood, and some even named the exact number of the house, and several callers said they remembered Kathy and her husband and son moving out of the place in a transit van. Two women told almost the same story about a further chilling appearance by the ghost in the summer of 1983. A single mother had moved into the house that year, and in July, her seven-year-old son, Martin, asked his mum if he could invite some of his friends from school to his birthday party. Five of Martin's cousins also attended the party, and so twelve children in total came to celebrate Martin's eighth birthday, and during the party, a clown turned up to entertain them. Martin's mother had not hired the clown, and assumed her mother Theresa had, but soon realised this was not the case at all. The clown shoved a slice of birthday cake into the face of one of the children, and then picked up a chair and threatened to smash it over Martin's head unless he sang 'Happy Birthday'. Children flew from the table in tears and ran into the kitchen to tell Martin's mum and another woman about the horrible clown, but when the women went into the living room, they saw the table tip over by itself, sending all of the food and drink everywhere. That night, Martin and his mother both heard someone sobbing in the bathroom, and whenever the bathroom door was opened, the crying sound would stop. As with Kathy and her family, Martin and his mother decided to move, and left within days. Martin stayed with his Nanny Theresa while his mother searched desperately for a flat to move into.

I have researched the case and to date, cannot find any clown who went under the name "Nobody" but I will keep looking and will hopefully try and get to the bottom of this intriguing but chilling case. At the time of writing the house said to be haunted by Nobody is unoccupied.

CLOSE ENCOUNTERS WITH ANGELS

In the winter months of 1984 going into 1985, the North West was the scene of one of the most inexplicable mysteries of all time, although it was only mentioned by the *Liverpool Echo* and Radio City. It all started about a week before Christmas, when scores of people from Llandudno, Wirral, Liverpool, Southport and Blackpool saw strange coloured lights flying across the skies. These lights were assumed to be UFOs by some and the authorities across the region blamed the planet Venus, which was visible low in the western skies at the time. Two Liverpool University security guards – Steve, aged 39, and George, aged 57, heard about the UFO reports on a Radio City news bulletin and also read about the sightings of the multicoloured lights that had now been seen over the city centre, close to the Royal Teaching Hospital. Steve was of the opinion that all of these sightings were mere misidentifications of the planet Venus, which looked like a very bright star at the time, but George shocked his younger colleague by stating that he had seen 'them' – and they were not UFOs. 'They were angels,' the guard had said. Steve thought George was pulling his leg at first, but George said he was deadly serious. He had been patrolling near Brownlow Hill around 2.30am and he had seen a light circling the University clock tower. It descended towards him and he could see a feminine-like figure, about 6 feet tall or more, hanging in the air, surrounded by an aura of rainbow light. George had been troubled by toothache at the time, but when he saw the figure the pain stopped and he was filled with a strange but uplifting feeling of peace and serenity. The figure then rose into the sky and went so high it became a star-like point. Around this time there was an intriguing report from several vagrants sleeping rough in St John's Gardens at the back of St George's Hall. The down and outs awoke around 3am to the sound of strange music – coming from above. They looked up and saw what they interpreted as a flight of angels – glowing men and women radiating gold, green, red and blue light, and they were singing harmoniously, hypnotically, in an unknown language. Waves of warm air evaporated the frost of the gardens, and the homeless people basked in the balmy localised climate, and some fell fast asleep. Steve, the University security guard, then heard a report of the angels from someone he could never doubt – his own mother, Peggy. She had been lying in her bed at a ward in the Royal Teaching Hospital, recovering from treatment for cervical cancer. She told her son that around 2.30am, a glowing woman had appeared at the window of her ward, even though she was about six storeys up. Peggy knew that the vision was of some angelic being, and in her mind, she heard the angel tell her not to worry about her condition because she'd soon be better. It also told her that her late husband would be reunited with her one day, and that he was always looking over her. Peggy's cancer then went into remission and she made a miraculous recovery. In the following month, on the night of Wednesday, 30 January 1985, the visitors from elsewhere were out in force across the North West, and this time Steve saw them himself as he did his rounds. Seven of them appeared high over Brownlow Hill, and the security guard decided to flash his torch up at them in a bid to attract their attention, and when he did, they flew down to him, scaring him at first – but he soon saw that these beings were beautiful and gave off a mesmerising multicoloured spectrum of light. In a whispering voice, Steve thanked the angels for saving his mum, and when they left after less than a minute, the guard found himself in tears. Not long after this, a woman who lost control of her car in icy weather and crashed on the M62 found herself trapped in the wreckage of her overturned vehicle before she passed out. Ambulance men found the woman thirty yards from her vehicle, and witnesses told how the woman had been lifted out of the car by 'glowing figures'. The woman could remember nothing, but later said she was visited one night as she recovered in hospital by two women who told her they had saved her so she could carry out 'good work'. The woman later joined a church group and devoted her life to charity work.

A CURIOUS CAVERN GHOST

Being interested in the supernatural, I am always intrigued when I hear of local ghostly goings-on and timeslips, especially when these paranormal incidents are alleged to have taken place in some of our well-known venues, and one of the most famous of these haunted locales is the Cavern. A ghost was said to have haunted the premises of the club in the late 1950s when it first opened as a jazz venue, and some "Cavern-Dwellers" even maintained that the Devil himself had occasionally put in an appearance at the most famous subterranean venue in the world from time to time. Why would the Fallen Angel manifest himself at a music venue of all places? I wondered, and two men at a Mathew Street café who had worked at the Cavern told me that the warehouse the club was located in had been built on the site of a strange underground temple created by the man Mathew

Street is named after - Mathew Pluckington, an incredibly successful and immensely wealthy Victorian merchant who was said to have dabbled with Devil-worship to prosper in his business dealings. True enough, a waterlogged vault, 120 feet long, 70 feet wide and about 9 feet in depth, was discovered directly beneath the stage where the Beatles had regularly performed at the Cavern when the club was being excavated in 1982. The purpose of this vault has never been explained, but this is just one of many Cavern mysteries I have collected over the years. Here's another one. At some time in November 1963, possibly just before the day JFK was assassinated, a promoter and a businessman were at the Cavern. Jimmy Tarbuck had done a stand-up comedy routine, and had been supported by a group known as Vic and the Spidermen. Sometime after the show, several people saw a green glowing light appear, and a businessman, who had been sitting in a corner, sipping a Coca Cola, saw a bizarre-looking figure appear in the green glare – an outlandishly-dressed girl with pink hair, a type of mini-skirt, black stockings and workman's boots. Her midriff was visible because she was wearing a revealing crop-top, and her bare lower back was adorned with some sort of oriental tattoo. This eccentric young lady had her hands clasped together and her eyes were closed as if he was in prayer. A promoter turned when the businessman cried out to him, and he got the closest view of the girl in the green light. He saw she had a ring in her nose and what was possibly a piercing in her bottom lip. A third person saw what was taken to be a ghost, and then, about 10 seconds after she appeared, the girl and the green luminescence vanished in an instant. The three men told no one else what they had seen, as they knew no one would believe them, and not long afterwards, the worrying news of President Kennedy's assassination soon eclipsed the memory of the strange ghostly girl, but decades later, one of these men later told me that he thought he had somehow seen a girl from some thirty or forty years away in the future – but why and how remains an inexplicable mystery. The ghostly girl's 'workingman's boots' had possibly been Doc Martens, and of course, the girls of this modern area are not averse to dying their hair pink and many wear tattoos and subject themselves to all sort of piercings in their faces and bodies. I wonder if some girl of today, perhaps in the 'new' Cavern Club, will somehow project herself back to that night in November 1963? It's a real puzzler.

ANOTHER ABDUCTION AT ST LUKE'S

Whenever Christmas is drawing near, a strange unearthly atmosphere descends upon the ruins of St Luke's – the "bombed-out church" as some call it, which has stood at the top of Bold Street since its completion in January 1831. It used to be a very popular church, but after it was left a burnt-out shell by a Nazi incendiary bomb in May 1941, many noticed the eerie atmosphere which took up residence in the shell of St Luke's. I have reports dating from the 1950s of ghostly shadowy figures being seen in the grounds and interior of the former church, and of strange chanting sounds and eerie organ music being heard in the vicinity of the ruin. Too many people have seen too many unfathomable things for it all to be in the mind, and these witnesses range from people passing St Luke's on their way to work during dark winter mornings, to police, and even prostitutes, who have encountered a recurring sinister figure time and time again: a tall man in black who wears a top hat. He has ink-black eyes and his height is estimated to be at least six feet and five inches. I feel that he was the ghost who returned a 6-year-old child named Abbi Edwards to her frantic family when she went missing near Bold Place one foggy December evening in 1991, just after the family had left their car to embark on a Christmas shopping trip. The family heard the girl's screams and realised they were coming from the interior of St Luke's but couldn't locate the hysterical child. The police were notified of the suspected abduction, but just as they were arriving at the church grounds, a tall man in black Victorian attire came through a door in the church and returned Abbi, and in a low creepy voice the backdated stranger intoned: "Please accept my sincere apology for any distress caused."

He then walked back into St Luke's but no one could find the door he had passed through, because it had been bricked up in the 1950s. Abbi said an old woman who 'looked like a witch' had grabbed her as she left the family car on Bold Place, and this stooped, bony-fingered woman had clamped her hand over Abbi's mouth before dragging her into St Luke's, where a very strange Mass took place. Abbi saw other terrified children dressed in modern clothes in the church, and a hooded man in black was doing handstands and carrying out what seemed to be a mocking parody of the Christian Mass on an altar. Abbi began to cry and the tall man in the topper wrenched the little girl from the old woman's clutches and returned her to the fogbound

Liverpool of the present. The policemen heard strange organ music coming from the supposedly empty church that December night, and even of a daytime, several people heard the perplexing piped music, including a woman who worked at the Leece Street job centre who had gone to sit on a bench at the back of the church to smoke a cigarette on her lunch break. These encounters with the ethereal inhabitants of St Luke's are mentioned in detail in *Haunted Liverpool* 4 and people who read my accounts of the ghostly goings-on in that book wrote to me in droves to tell me of their own experiences. One of the most chilling encounters with the top-hatted man in black apparently took place one foggy night in the late 1980s, when a 19-year-old student named Hattie left a wine bar on Hardman Street in a drunken state and collapsed near the gates of St Luke's. Hattie's friend, Jenny went in search of her, and saw the tall silhouette of a man pick Hattie up and walk off into the mists towards the church grounds. Jenny alerted a nearby policeman on his beat about the incident, and this constable immediately entered the grounds of St Luke's with a flashlight – and soon noticed lights in the windows of the derelict church. The policeman then spotted a tall man who looked as if he was in fancy dress and make-up because he wore a top hat, a long black coat, and the eyes of this peculiar man were black, with no white in them. In his arms he held an unconscious teenage girl. Three times the policeman ordered the stranger to put the girl down but he stood there stock-still, saying nothing, when all of a sudden he dropped Hattie onto the grass.

He then floated steadily and silently away into the depths of the fog and vanished. Just what the ghost intended to do to the student is a mystery, as is the identity of the apparition.

One bitterly cold night in January 1991, a 22-year-old student named Rob left a pub on Renshaw Street and walked up Leece Street on his way to his home (which was a student flat off Caledonia Street). As he neared the corner of Roscoe Street and Leece Street, Rob noticed a group of men of around his age, all standing at the railings that enclose St Luke's Church. The men were all watching something in silence, and Rob went to see what it was. When he looked through the railings he could hardly believe his eyes. In the grassy grounds of the derelict church, two tall figures in top hats and long coats were holding the hands of about a dozen or more children aged perhaps around 9 or 10, and these children formed a chain as they held hands with one another in a perfect circle. The circle of children and the two weirdly dressed adults were rotating as if their feet were not touching the ground at quite a speed. Rob swore and asked what was going on and a man turned to him briefly and said, 'They've been doing it for about half an hour,' then looked back at the unearthly spectacle. Then there came exclamations of astonishment and swear words as the circle of figures faded away into nothing. Rob stood there for some time, and so did a few others, hoping to see what had obviously been ghosts, return for an encore, but they never did, and Rob struck up a friendship with one of the witnesses that morning and later married his sister.

Today, the two men often talk about the eerie scene that greeted their eyes that wintry morning, and now, in the light of all the reports I have unearthed regarding St Luke's, they feel more comfortable talking to other people about the incident.

STALKED BY DEATH

The following story was told me a few years ago after I delivered a well-attended talk on the supernatural at a library in Wirral. One frosty grey afternoon in the January of 1977, a small-time criminal named Marty was driving along Queen's Drive Wavertree, homeward bound for his home in Kirkby, when he noticed a hearse passing by on his left. The Coffin the hearse was carrying was almost obscured by five letters made of yellow and white flowers which spelt out the word "MARTY" – and this sent a chill down Marty's spine, but then he saw the cars following the hearse, and he couldn't believe his eyes, because the funeral cortege was made up of two black limousines and six other cars of various colours and makes, and Marty knew all of the people in these cars. His old mother had been in the first limo, and in the cars that followed, the criminal had seen his brother-in-law and several people he hadn't seen for years. The hearse and train of cars full of mourners went through the roundabout, and Marty almost crossed the give-way line at the same roundabout as he tried to follow the eerie hearse. By the time he got through the roundabout the funeral car and the uncanny entourage were nowhere to be seen. When Marty reached his home in Southdene he told his wife Janet about the hearse with his name on and how he had even seen her brother as well as his own mother in the limos, but Janet said it had just been some other Marty and the people had looked like his mother and her brother. Marty shook his head and gazed out the window with a far-away look in his eyes. He was sure that the hearse had been some omen of death, and he had the unsettling feeling that he would come to a sticky end some day soon. Marty saw it as payback for all the bad things he had done to people over the years; all of those houses he had robbed, stretching back to his teenage years. He particularly remembered the morning he had even stolen the presents from under a Christmas tree, and he recalled how upset the family had been when they realised they had been broken into early that Christmas morn. Marty confessed to this crime and others to his wife and Janet said he should go and see a priest, but Marty sank into a depression. He went to his local pub that evening, and as he sat in front of the open fire, an old man pointed to the flames and said, 'Hey, doesn't that piece of coal look like a coffin?' Marty looked and saw that the piece was indeed shaped just like a coffin, and he saw this as yet another omen of impending death.

Marty stayed in the pub until long after midnight, and the landlord had a 'stay-behind' – also known as a 'lock-in' – where the doors of the pub are locked so no one can get into the pub after hours, and hopefully any policeman would also be unable to enter the pub, which was breaking the law by staying open so late. The time was almost 2.20am, and eleven customers were enjoying the after-hours session. Marty went into the pub toilets, and found himself alone as he stood before the urinal. He stood there swaying slightly, and he could hear people chatting, laughing and singing in the parlour. After a few moments he went to the wash-basin to rinse his hands, and then he headed towards the door – but suddenly found his way barred by what Marty could only describe as a solid shadow. The tall black silhouette of a man stood there, and Marty just knew that it was some personification of death. He stopped in his tracks and then backed away from the apparition. He was so afraid, he ran into a toilet cubicle and locked the door, then climbed up onto the cistern and tried to open the window. Being an expert housebreaker, he performed a certain trick of his trade to open the small window, and then he slid out this window head-first, and landed in the yard of the public house, almost breaking his arm. A huge Alsatian dog that had been put in the yard to guard the premises then attacked Marty and tore his sleeve and bit his forearm. Marty climbed up onto a dustbin and somehow managed to climb over the wall and drop into the entry. He reached his home in a terrible state, and despite Jan's advice for him to go to hospital to get a tetanus injection for the dog bite, Marty stayed up, drank half a bottle of whiskey, and then went to bed around 5.30am.

A few days after this, Jan fell ill and went to see her doctor. It turned out she was pregnant, but Marty believed he would never see his son or daughter's birth, because he was convinced he was being stalked by death. For the first time in almost twenty-five years he went into St Chad's and prayed. He promised God he'd change his ways now, and even decided he'd somehow trace the family he had stolen the Christmas presents from, all those years ago, and anonymously mail them as much money as he could save. He left the church and went home, and although he felt the urge to go to the pub, he watched television instead and helped Jan with her household chores, and then he went for a long walk around half-past eleven. At the lonely junction of Simonswood Lane and Quarryside Drive, Marty stopped to have a cigarette, and as he lit up, he felt something cold touch his left shoulder. It was a jet-black hand, and Marty knew that hand belonged to Death. Marty froze, afraid to turn to face his Nemesis, for he wasn't ready to leave his life, now that he was about to become a father, and the hand gripped hard on his shoulder and seemed to be trying to turn him round. But Marty spat out the cigarette, and walked forward, whispering the Lord's Prayer as he did. He was surprised he knew the words to a prayer he had not recited since he was a schoolboy. He could see the grotesque and freakish long shadow of the thing following him on the ground as he walked down Simonswood Lane, but

Marty kept reciting the Lord's Prayer, and eventually the shadow vanished, and he glanced once over his shoulder to see that the thing had gone. When he came home, he emptied the remains of the whiskey into the kitchen sink and vowed he would truly turn over a new leaf in his godforsaken life. He devoted his life from that moment on to charity work, and today he is a proud grandfather, still living in Kirkby, and still doing good turns for the disadvantaged of his community. 'It's never too late to make a new start in life,' Marty told me, 'and I feel as if I was reborn when I went straight.'

Many people, including some famous ones, have expressed the belief that death was stalking them. John Lennon is a case in point. In fact there were a host of strange incidents surrounding John's death. On the evening of Wednesday, 11 April 1962, John had recently arrived in Germany to see his friend and Beatles bassist Stu Sutcliffe, only to discover that he had just died from a brain haemorrhage. John went on stage, but before the performance he made a very cryptic announcement: "Stuart Sutcliffe was a very special human being, and a remarkable man. He once told me that he had the ability to see into the future, and I for one now believe that Stu was telling the truth." What had happened to cause Lennon to say this? We will probably never know, and it continues to vex Beatle biographers to this day, but some close to Lennon claimed Sutcliffe had predicted global Beatlemania of religious magnitude, but had added he would not live to see the phenomenal success himself. Some versions of this (possible) myth say Stu had also predicted just twenty years of fame for John before he met his Nemesis. In 1976, former Beatles roadie Mal Evans was shot dead by Los Angeles police officers who mistook Mal's air rifle for a real firearm during a domestic incident, and Lennon, upon hearing of Mal's death, stated: 'I'll be next, I just know it,' and talked about being stalked by 'the Angel of Death'. Shortly before Lennon was murdered, two unexplained incidents took place; a psychic named Alex Tanous was asked to make a prediction for NBC's 'Unexplained Phenomena Show' and in reply said: 'A very famous foreign-born rock star will have an untimely death and this can happen from this moment on. I say untimely because there is something strange about his death, but it will affect the consciousness of many people because of his fame.' As he made the prediction, Tanous looked out the windows of the New York venue – over to the Dakota Apartments, where Lennon was living at that time with wife Yoko and son Sean. There is also a lesser-known paranormal incident foreshadowing Lennon's death; Just after Angela Ripon read the news on BBC1 on 9 December 1980, a brief newsflash about Lennon's murder came on the screen, followed by the play, *The Flipside of Dominic Hide* - which was about a time-traveller from the future. People eagerly switched over to *News At Ten* that evening but were baffled at learning nothing further of such a world-shaking tragedy. Most reports of the 'phantom' news bulletin came from Merseyside, and were never explained. I have asked people who saw the newsflash if they were getting their dates mixed up, but all were certain it had been the night before Lennon's untimely end. They say approaching tragedies often cast their shadows before them.

President Kennedy apparently thought death was stalking him in the months leading up to his shocking fate in Dallas, and he is said to have visited the Pope, perhaps to receive a special blessing, because he thought the end was near. He said to his wife Jackie at one point, just before he went to Dallas, that: 'if someone wants to shoot me with a rifle from a window, there's nothing I can do about it, so why worry?' and Jackie Kennedy went cold when her husband uttered this prophetic line. Several mediums at the time, including Jean Dixon, all reported having visions of JFK's assassination, but no one acted upon them, as far as I know. A century before, Abraham Lincoln had a well-documented lucid dream that his own body was laying in a coffin at the White House, just before he was assassinated. Some people close to Marc Bolan said the glam-rock star was apparently under the impression that he would soon die in some tragedy, and is said to have remarked to a friend: 'If I died now I wouldn't even make page 3 news.' Days later he died when his mini crashed into a tree.

THE MEN IN BLACK

One sunny Saturday afternoon in November 1978, a 27-year-old woman named June was gazing idly out the window of her flat on the thirteenth floor of Crosbie Heights, off Everton's William Henry Street, when she noticed something odd, high up in the blue sky – a little white triangle with rounded corners – and it was hovering there, stationary. June thought it looked the same shape as a triangular foil-wrapped Dairylea cheese segment. She shouted to her husband George – who was watching a Rugby League match on the telly – to come and look at the strange craft. George saw the UFO too and rummaged about in a sideboard for his old bird-watching binoculars. The craft had vanished by the time George had taken the binoculars out the case, but June used them to survey the skies for a while – and she spotted not one, but three of white triangular craft, flying in a row as they descended from the blue.

George had gone for cigarettes and the pink sports Echo by now, and June wished he'd hurry back so she could show him the strange objects that were descending onto the waterfront. Then she had a funny turn. June felt dizzy and then nauseous, and she ran to the toilet to be sick. George then returned and when June said she'd been sick all of a sudden, he told her to lie down. At this time, June noticed that the binoculars had gone missing. She and George looked high and low for them but never found them or their leather case and lens caps. On the following day, George was on his way to work on his motorbike when he had a serious crash which left him in hospital. Something unexplained took place at this well-known hospital shortly after the crash. George was laying in the hospital bed in traction, with weights hanging from frames, pins in his legs, and a plaster-cast on his arm. When June went to visit him, she discovered that George's bed was empty and no one knew where he was. The patient obviously hadn't been discharged nor could he have discharged himself, for he was dosed with morphine and unable to move anyway with pins in the bones of his legs. The traction weights rested on pulleys around the empty bed, but George was nowhere to be seen. That evening at 9.10pm, George was found tucked into his hospital bed and unable to say where he had been. He recalled nothing to explain his whereabouts. June then began to recall what had happened that Saturday when she had become ill after watching the triangular UFOs. She had heard a cough to her left as she was looking through the binoculars at the strange craft, and she had turned to see a tall black man, dressed all in black, and was naturally startled by his presence. In a low voice devoid of any accent, the stranger told June to say nothing about the UFOs she had just seen – 'Or we'll take you away and no one will ever see you again,' he had threatened. That's all June could remember. Had this man taken her binoculars? Years later June read about the mysterious 'men in black' who often turn up to harass witnesses who have seen UFOs. Had the man who appeared in her living room been one of these, and had he something to do with George's inexplicable disappearance and reappearance at the hospital?

The men in black figure in the following account, which features another aspect of the UFO phenomenon – the USO – an abbreviation for Unidentified Submarine Object.

On the morning of Tuesday, 20 November 1979, at 1.40am, a 24-year-old man from Prenton on the Wirral named Stuart arrived at the Albert Dock, which in those days lay derelict and deserted. Stuart had spent the earlier part of the evening in Kirklands wine bar and restaurant on Hardman Street with his friends, before going on to a club on Victoria Street. When he emerged from the club at one in the morning, he saw that Liverpool was still blanketed by a thick fog which now seemed even worse. Visibility had dropped to less than twenty feet. The Liverpool and Manchester airports were closed because of the fog, and flights had to be transferred to other airports. Police closed both carriageways of the M62 over a 15-mile stretch from the Liverpool exit to allow salvage and rescue work to continue after more than twenty serious fog-related crashes occurred on the motorway. Stuart soldiered on through the freezing fog, and being fitter than most people (because he was a body-building enthusiast who exercised with weights four hours each day) he whistled as he located the old rowing boat in the crumbling rat-infested dock warehouse. The boat was slid over a quayside, causing an almighty splash in the calm waters. Stuart then went down the quayside steps and carefully boarded the old boat he and his friends had repaired. He began to row, despite being slightly intoxicated, and at one point in the middle of the river he took off his coat because he sweated so much. Three quarters into the 1,300 yard journey to Woodside (where the boat would be tethered at the quayside of another abandoned dock), the streetlamps of Birkenhead could be seen as faint pinpoints of light through the fog, but there was another source of illumination nearby, and Stuart could see it was coming from under the Mersey. He stopped rowing, and saw a glowing green disk-shaped object about ten feet below the surface. The centre of this luminous green disk pulsated with a bright white light. As the young man knelt and leaned over the side of the boat, he saw the disk had about sixteen circular features around its rim – and they started to spin as he looked on. Spokes of light also radiated from the central glowing disk as the mysterious craft rotated. The unidentified submarine object (USO) then moved steadily away, northwards, towards the estuary, and the motion of the object created a current in the waters which turned the rowing boat around. Stuart rowed like mad, fearing the boat would capsize, and soon reached his destination. He climbed up the moss-coated waterfront steps and headed home. On the following morning the rowing boat was still there but someone spotted it and reported it to the authorities. Stuart made no further illegal nocturnal crossings. The unknown craft Stuart encountered was seen by many people throughout the late 1970s and early 1980s in the Mersey, Liverpool Bay and beyond. Sometimes these USOs would surface and fly off silently into the night-time sky, and in 1981 scores of people in Crosby saw such a craft do this. Around this time, a number of trawlers from Ireland were dragged under the waves of the Irish Sea by nuclear subs that had become entangled in their nets. Questions were asked in Parliament about all the sub activity in the Irish Sea, and the Admiralty claimed a propeller had fallen off a sub (which was powered by two nuclear reactors) and this vessel had to be towed to Holy Loch for repairs, but strange rumours then circulated about an underwater 'UFO base' that was being investigated by the military. We may one day know the truth. About a week after Stuart had glimpsed the circular USO in the Mersey, he was contacted at his home by telephone by a man who called himself Captain Moore, who claimed he was based at the Admiralty building near the Liver Buildings. Moore said he had learned of Stuart's encounter with the craft during his illegal crossing, and intended to report the matter to the police and the Ministry of Defence, and this naturally alarmed Stuart. Captain Moore then said he was willing to stay quiet about the matter if Stuart would do the same. Stuart became suspicious at this stipulation and wondered if a friend was playing a prank on him, but he agreed to Captain Moore's terms. For the next three months, Stuart and his parents heard strange clicks and faint voices on their telephone, which was, of course, in 1979, a landline. During this period when the phone was apparently bugged, a neighbour living next door to Stuart said two men in military uniforms had visited the house while Stuart and his parents were at work, and they had evidently possessed a key to the premises, because the neighbour had seen them walking about in the front parlour and leaving the house via the backyard door. Then a chilling incident took place a few days after this, when Stuart was walking to a friend's flat in Liverpool. He left Lime Street Station, walked up Mount Pleasant, and was just about to cross over the road into Hope Street when a police car pulled up in front of him at the kerb. Two policemen asked Stuart what his name was and if he had ever been in trouble with the police. Stuart gave the requested details and stated that he had never been in trouble with the law in his life. All the same, the policemen told him to get into the back of their car, and Stuart reluctantly did. They then drove down Orford Street and parked around a secluded corner just a stone's throw from the old Irish Centre, on Duckinfield Street, behind the Metropolitan Cathedral. Here, the 'policeman' quizzed Stuart about the thing he had seen under the Mersey, and only then did he realise that the inquisitors were not policemen at all, but something else. At first he thought that they were perhaps some intelligence agents connected to the shady Captain Moore, but Stuart noticed, at close quarters, that the two men's faces looked odd. They seemed to be wearing make-up and lipstick, which did not make sense at all, but the young man felt very unnerved by the appearance of the questioners. Stuart asked to be released, but one of the fake policemen warned him: 'If you breathe a word of your experience about the thing in the river, we will know, believe us, we will know, and we will have you taken away. You will never see your parents or anyone else you know ever again. They will still be looking for you in a hundred years time.'

The bogus policemen then let Stuart go and he rushed from the vehicle, thoroughly shaken by the threats. He had only reached the corner of the street about thirty yards away, when he looked back – and the police car and its sinister occupants had vanished. Fearing he would be 'taken away' by the unearthly duo, Stuart said nothing more about the USO in case the mysterious men returned to apprehend him, and only told me about his encounter with the underwater UFO in 2009 when I mentioned similar sights of USOs in the Merseyside area on a radio programme. A man who worked on the Liverpool ferries in the 1960s also got in touch to tell me of the strange green lights he and other people saw at night under the Mersey between 1961 and 1968. This man also spoke of phonecalls made to his home in the dead of night after he had told a friend in a pub about the lights in the river. The caller would say nothing, and hang up after about a minute. It's possible that these were just crank calls, but in the light of Stuart's experiences, we must remain open-minded to the possibility that the men in black were menacing a witness. From the mid-1960s to the 1980s, there were hundreds of sightings of UFOs emerging and diving into the sea off the coast of Brazil, and on 30 July 1967, officers and crew of an Argentinian ship called *Naviero* watched in disbelief as an unidentified cigar-shaped craft, over a 100 feet in length, cruised beside their vessel without leaving a wake in the waters. This happened 120 miles from the Brazilian coast. Captain Julian Ardanza came up onto the deck of the *Naviero* and saw the unidentified sub for himself and it was quite clearly like no submarine made on earth, for it had no conning tower, and its hull glowed with a blue light. The sub suddenly dived into the depths at an amazing speed. The captain had seen nothing like this in all of his two decades at sea. More than seventy per cent of this planet is covered by water, and the average depth of our oceans is about two miles, and most of this vast underwater world is unexplored. Any spacefaring race that can travel light years to our world would have no difficulty building bases in our ocean depths for whatever reasons they might have, be it simply the establishment of a base for surveillance programmes or, God forbid, a base for some future military campaign against us.

WHO HAUNTED WHOM?

Early one wintry Saturday morning in the 1950s, Charles, the managing director of a certain well-known Liverpool store, was walking through Sefton Park with Sid, a friend from his childhood days, when Charles suddenly asked him if he believed in ghosts. 'No, why?' Sid replied with a curious look. 'Oh, nothing,' said Charles, and he attempted to smile. That night he called Sid just after midnight and said a naked woman was in his flat. Sid was lost for words. Charles said he had heard the bath running and went to see what was going on, and he saw a naked lady testing the bathwater with her toes. 'She's got to be a ghost, obviously,' bachelor

Charles whispered into the mouthpiece, 'unless she has a key to my flat. Remember I lost my keys last year?'

Sid reminded Charles that he'd had the locks changed, then said: 'Cor, I wouldn't mind a naked Judy haunting my pad.' And there was a pause. Charles said he had looked into the bathroom and now the woman had gone – and the bath was bone dry. He also said he thought he had seen the same woman standing in his kitchen the week before, but she had vanished after a few seconds. Sid advised his friend to get some shut-eye and advised him to book a holiday somewhere nice and warm, adding: 'They'll manage perfectly well at that store without you for a week or so, mate.'

On the following night at 10pm, Charles saw the same ghostly woman walk into his living room with a towel wound around her head, and one wrapped about her torso. She stood before the fire and gazed into the mirror above it – then began to say something to her reflection in words that sounded French.

'Excuse me!' Charles shouted, and when he could not attract the lady's attention, he telephoned Sid, and said: 'Get over here now and you can see her for yourself. She's here again and she's no ghost!'

Sid only lived a short distance from his friend's flat near Sefton Park, and he drove over, full of curiosity and a little fearful too, but when he arrived the lady had vanished, although Sid could smell a sweet feminine type of perfume in the air.

'When she saw me she ran into the bedroom screaming – and then – she was gone! Like that!'

Charles clicked his fingers. At 3am, Charles got out of bed to go the toilet, and as he passed his living room he looked in and saw a coffin standing on a bier. He squeezed his eyes, looked again – and now the coffin and its stand had gone. Charles went cold and wondered why he was seeing all of these strange things. A week later, Charles suffered a fatal heart attack at work. His coffin was placed in his living room prior to burial for the wake, and a month later, a French teacher in her twenties moved into the deceased's former flat. She left after seeing the ghost of a man who would appear and stare at her. She first saw him as she was getting out of her bath, but the final straw came one night when he shouted something at her and chased her into the bedroom. The French tutor fainted, and moved out soon after. When Sid heard about this he felt a shiver down his spine. Sid is in his eighties now, and remembers this strange incident quite clearly, and afterwards he asked me, 'Who haunted who?' And I confessed I wasn't at all sure at all; it seems to have all been the result of some slippage in time perhaps, with the future and past overlapping. That's the only way I can explain it.

DREAMS OF MURDER

Albert Einstein advanced physics with his theories and equations, but no one has come along to further our understanding of the mind. Main de Biran, Schopenhauer, Bergson, Freud and Jung have offered their interesting hypotheses, but all of these thinkers did not back up their theories with any scientific proof. An Einstein of psychology who can scientifically explain the workings of the mind is long overdue, and such a genius might be able to throw some light on those mysterious forms of mental activity – dreams.

The average sleeper has 3 to 5 dreams per night, and while most dreams can be nothing more than surreally-tinted expressions of wish fulfilment or confrontation of a deeply-held fear (in the form of a nightmare), some dreams seem to be psychic in nature. The Bible and other archaic texts are full of prophecies that are received during sleep, and I have collected over 450 local dreams of apparent prophecies from local people over the years. It seems that the mind can, in certain states of altered consciousness, not only open up the future, it can also view incidents in the present that are taking place many miles away, and the following account is a case in point. One humid evening in June, 1959, a man in his thirties named John returned to his Kensington home after taking his wife Ann in to Oxford Street Maternity Hospital. Ann was due to give birth to her first child within a few days, and it was a very nervous time for the couple. John did some DIY at his home to take his mind off his worries regarding his pregnant wife. He laid a carpet in the hall, and then he started to paint the kitchen cupboards, but by midnight, he felt exhausted, and decided to have a bath before retiring to bed. As he lay in bed, he worried about his wife in her heavily-pregnant condition, and wished she was beside him as he began to fall asleep. John then had a strange dream about a sinister-looking man about the same age as himself. This man was strangling a young woman who fell to her knees as she struggled – in vain – to get free of the killer's hands. After the despicable act, the killer placed the partially-clothed corpse in a sitting position beneath a tree – then turned to face John, as if he could see him, and grinned. John woke up in a sweat with a pounding heart. The dream was so vivid it stuck in John's mind for years. Then, in November 1963, the murderer returned to haunt the dreams of John, and again he strangled the victim before stripping off all of her clothes, and on this occasion he also extracted the young woman's teeth with what looked like a pair of pliers. The dream was so vivid, John could hear the ghastly sound of the teeth being wrenched out. Once again the strangler turned to face John and smiled. Months after this, Ann shook her husband awake one night after hearing him shouting in his sleep. John woke up with a look of horror on his face. He had experienced another lucid dream of murder, and again the strangler was seen to gruesomely remove teeth from his victim with pliers. He had also seen the killer stuff the victim's underwear deep into her mouth for some sadistic reason. John had eight of these dreams, and after the seventh dream, in the autumn of 1964, something terrifying took place. John was in Blacklers, buying a present for his wife's birthday, when he suddenly had the unnerving feeling that he was being watched. He just felt as if someone's eyes were on him all the time. He turned – and saw him – the murderer from the graphic recurring nightmares. There was no doubt about it – this was the very man he had seen in his stomach-churning dreams of murder. This ominous smartly-dressed stranger stood there staring at John with an expressionless face, as if he knew him. John was stunned, and he hurried away to a counter to pay for the present – and the eerie man from his dreams followed. John left the store with a sense of mounting panic, and upon reaching the corner of Ranelagh Street, he halted and pretended to look into the window of H Samuel the jewellers, but instead he looked through the window pane into Charlotte Street – and saw the 'killer' heading towards him at a brisk pace. John hailed a hackney cab, and the weird man came right up to the taxi door and looked in at John as he got in the vehicle.

'Where to mate?' the cabby asked.

'Kensington,' John mumbled. He was scared of the weirdo hearing his address.

'Yeah, what part of Kensington, mate? Can you speak up?' the taxi driver asked with a bemused expression.

John told the cabby to take him to a street in Old Swan instead, but when the taxi got as far as Brownlow Hill, John told the cabby to take him to the street in Kensington where he lived instead. All the way to his home, John sat in the taxi, trying to fathom out how he had been dreaming of a man who actually existed. Was the man somehow connected to him? John could not think of any connection, and when he told his wife about the frightening incident, she said the stranger had just resembled the man he had dreamt about, but John knew that wasn't the case at all, but he couldn't understand what was going on.

John had the final dream about the strangler in February of the following year – and this time he realised he had somehow been seeing the so-called "Jack the Stripper" murders – committed from 1959 onwards by a man who strangled and stripped his victims in London. He also removed some of the teeth of his eight victims to keep as grisly trophies. Were John's dreams just vivid, grisly nightmares, or, during sleep, did he somehow tune in to the mind of "Jack the Stripper"? Many of the victims had local connections; one was born in Bebington, whilst others had plied their trade in the city. The murderer was never brought to justice and the case remains unsolved. In my book *Murders On Merseyside*, there is a chapter entitled "Two Visions of Death" in which I have detailed two extraordinary well-documented and well-witnessed prophecies of murder with a local connection. In May 1812, a Mr John Williams, a wealthy banker of Redruth, Cornwall, had a number of vivid nightmares in which he saw the Prime Minister Spencer Percival being assassinated by a tall man who stepped out from behind a pillar to shoot him. Another man, who has never been named, also recorded the very same nightmare up in Scotland, and sure enough on Monday 11 May of that year, Spencer Percival was assassinated by a 42-year-old bankrupt Liverpool businessman named John Bellingham who stepped out from behind a pillar in the House of Commons and shot the Prime Minister dead. The second instance of a murder being seen before it occurred is also mentioned in the chapter, and this is the amazing prophecy that was made by the late psychic Alex Tanous in September 1980. Tanous was asked to make a prediction live on air as he was being interviewed by Lee Spiegel of NBC radio's *Unexplained Phenomena Show*. Tanous seemed to go into a trance as he looked out the windows of the office where the interview was being held. He gazed over at the Dakotas, a block of luxury penthouses where New York's glitterati lived, and the medium said: 'A very famous rock star will have an untimely death, and this can happen from this moment on. I say "untimely" because there is something strange about this death, but it will affect the consciousness of many people because of his fame. The star will be foreign-born but living in the United States.'

And of course, the rest is tragic history which did

indeed affect the consciousness of millions of people across the world. A few months after the prophecy of death by Tanous, John Lennon was shot as he walked through the archway leading to his home – at the Dakotas – the very block Tanous had been gazing at when he made his grim prediction. The assassin who shot John in the back was Mark David Chapman, who is still behind bars today. Tanous never explained what he meant by there being 'something strange' about the killing though. Some conspiracy theorists have conjectured that the politically active Lennon was seen as a threat to the reactionary policies of newly-elected President Ronald Reagan, and so, the globally famous singer, famed for such highly-motivational political songs as *Give Peace A Chance* and *Power to the People*, was 'removed' by the CIA, who may have killed Lennon with a trained assassin lurking in the shadows near to an unwitting Chapman. I have looked into this killing in some depth and believe there was no such conspiracy. In my opinion, Chapman shot Lennon because he was insane, and allegedly saw John as a manipulative "phoney" who talked about imagining "no possessions" in his atheistic utopian classic *Imagine* – whilst living a life of luxury in a top-class penthouse with millions in the bank.

MYSTERIES OF THE
SPACE-TIME CONTINUUM

A few years ago I gave an illustrated lecture on the topic of time travel, and in the midst of the talk, I claimed that Leonardo da Vinci, a genius centuries ahead of his time, had designed robots amongst the other inventions he created, and a man attending the talk called me a liar. In reply I laid down a challenge: he was to give me a thousand pounds or withdraw his comment, for I could prove my claims, as far-fetched as they seemed. The heckler wouldn't withdraw, so I had him promise, before witnesses, that he would pay a thousand pounds to charity if I could prove my claim, and prove it I did, by showing him a copy of the *Codex Atlanticus*, an ancient voluminous manuscript showing the red chalk sketches of a robotic knight, actually created by Leonardo at Milan in 1495 – the very first humanoid robot in the history of Western civilization. The heckler made himself scare and never paid up.

Was Leonardo some stranded time traveller from the future? Probably not, but I sometimes wonder if he was able to see into the future in some psychic capacity. Do time-travellers exist? I've met a few alleged travellers over the years, some were charlatans or delusional but I'm not so sure about a few others I've met. At a book-signing in 2008 a shaven-headed man in a red Adidas tracksuit named Jason – who hailed from Knowlsley - told me nonchalantly he was working on a time machine. A relative had won the lottery and given him 'a few bob' and now he was building a machine that could travel haphazardly through time. People around Jason laughed, but this man knew about the Casimir Effect, Cerenkov radiation, quantum oscillators, the ins and out of the Copenhagen Interpretation, as well as various other advanced technical aspects of modern physics which convinced me that he did have an in-depth knowledge of hypothetical time travel and quantum mechanics. Jason said he had made two trips into the future and had seen wide-scale rioting and 'some sort of revolution' in progress – including the shooting of a Prime Minister. He also claimed that he had arrived at some period in what looked like the not-too-distant future and found that most of the city centre of Liverpool had been laid waste. Both cathedrals were in ruins, and the distinctive St John's Beacon had toppled and crashed onto Clayton Square. Ominous palls of white smoke covered the Mersey and Wirral looked like Hiroshima with hardly a building standing. Not a living soul was to be seen anywhere and not a single sound of a bird could be heard. Jason showed me what were alleged to be images of this grim desolation on his phone; if they were not photoshopped then we may be in store for some nasty surprises in the future.

People sniggered at Jason's claims, and smirking faces peeped over his shoulder when he unfolded the schematic plans to his 'time machine' on the table. 'The neodymium torus magnet was the most expensive part of the machine,' Jason told me, sliding the blueprint across the table, but a store guard moved him on, saying people were waiting to have their books signed. I later received an email from Jason, dated Tuesday 11 August 2015, saying he had built the machine and was now seven years in the future. Of course, any hacker could date an email like that, so the jury is still out regarding Jason, but I have a strange feeling about the alleged Knowsley time-traveller.

Continuing our subject of time-travel and timeslips, in 2011 I interviewed a 72-year-old Huyton lady named Margaret, who clearly recalled a very strange man who accosted her as a 6-year-old girl on Scotland Road in 1946 – and showed her what looked exactly like a modern iPhone of today. Margaret noticed the man, who was in his thirties, taking pictures with the peculiar device of the site where the Rotunda Theatre stood before it was destroyed in the May Blitz of 1941. Margaret asked the man what he was doing and he took her picture with the tiny flat box. When Margaret told her uncle Jim (who was an amateur photographer) about the man, he said the box had been some sort of light meter, but Margaret is adamant that the man held a modern-day touch-screen iPhone. Was this man a time traveller? On YouTube there is clear footage of a woman using another anachronistic mobile phone at a 1928 premiere of a Charlie Chaplin film. Google "Charlie Chaplin time traveller" and see her for yourself.

There have been some intriguing time-slips in the Kirkby area recently. Two sisters in their thirties named Lisa and Angela told me how, one Spring day in 2009, they went to Kirkby town centre to shop and saw a delightful shop that sold wool. The women were pushed for time and decided they'd both go back to the quaint premises, which was called "Bennet's Wool Shop" – but in the following week they could not find the shop in question and made enquiries at a few other shops in the area. One shopkeeper the sisters talked to said a 'Bennet's Wool Shop' had once existed in the exact place as the shop which Lisa and Angela visited, but it had closed down some years ago. This really shook the girls up and they slowly realised they had experienced a timeslip. An elderly couple from Kirkby's Northwood area wrote to me a few years back to say how, one summer's morning in the 1970s, they were walking down Old Hall Lane, enjoying the sunshine. Margy was 27 at the time and she pushed her year-old child in a buggy as her husband Billy walked proudly alongside her. Margy glanced over the low wall of St Chad's churchyard and saw a funeral taking place. Nothing strange about that you may think, but the priest and the mourners were all dressed in old-fashioned clothes, and Margy notice a female mourner who wore a huge black bonnet and a black mantilla lace veil covering her face as she sobbed. The woman's into-the-waist jacket and the dress that went down to her boots were black, as were the clothes of the mourners. The men held straw boater hats in their hands as they gazed with bowed heads towards the open grave, and all of these men had centre-parted hair-cuts and distinctive moustaches that looked waxed. The priest wore a strange looking hat and he halted the graveside prayer as he noticed the couple walking past. Billy halted and gazed at the outdated figures, but Margy, sensing the people were ghosts, grabbed her husband's arm and dragged him along with her. Moments later, the figures were nowhere to be seen. Margy was convinced the phantom funeral was some omen and expected to hear of a death, but thankfully she never did. Margy did not know at the time that this phantom funeral had been seen by many other locals over the years, but no one knows whose burial is taking place in what seems to be a recurring time-slippage to the Victorian or Edwardian era.

One of the most intriguing and downright sinister timeslip incidents that came my way concerns the reports made to me by two retired policemen named Ian and Gary. In the 1970s, Ian and Gary were on patrol in the Toxteth and Edge Hill areas of Liverpool, and one summer night around 10.40pm they received a report over the radio from the police control room; a number of passers-by had heard a violent domestic at a house at the northern end of Grove Street, not far from a disused church. Both policemen knew the area of Edge Hill well and knew beyond a shadow of a doubt that there was no such house standing in that area of Grove Street because there was only a rectangle of grass between St Stephen's Church and the Oxford public house, close to the University campus. That rectangle of greenery had resulted from the wholesale demolition of terraced houses that lined Grove Street in the 1960s. The radio operator then said she had just that minute had another call from a woman who lived on Smithdown Lane who had just heard 'blue murder' at the house on Grove Street, and terrible screams. Ian and Gary therefore drove from Toxteth's Selborne Street to the alleged scene of the domestic, determined to prove that the reports were bogus, but when they reached the northern end of Grove Street the policemen were startled to see a two storey house standing on its own, about fifty feet from the disused church. Ian looked at Gary and said, 'When did that go up?' Neither of the two constables had seen that house there before this night, and were baffled by its presence.

Gary got out the car to take a closer look. The number on the door was 35, and through the bay windows, he and his colleague could see a lamp of some sort which threw enough light into the parlour to show them that no one was present. Gary knocked heavily three times at the door, but received no reply. Ian decided to try the doorknob and turned it to discover that the front door was unlocked. A sweet sickly aroma similar to cinnamon greeted the noses of the coppers as they entered the hallway.

'Anyone home?' Ian shouted as he looked up the dark stairs. He looked for a light switch but couldn't find one. Gary looked into the parlour but didn't enter it. He and Ian switched on their torches and went into the kitchen, and here they came upon a bizarre and creepy sight. A naked woman was sitting at the kitchen table in the dark. Again, Ian looked for a light switch but saw there was none. He said to the seated nude, 'Alright love?'

But there was no reply and not a flicker of any reaction from the woman. She did not even squint when the torches were shone in her face. Gary touched her forearm and it felt cold. The skin didn't feel right, and then Ian touched the woman's shoulder and her face. Stone cold. Immediately the policemen thought the worst – that the woman had been murdered and left in the sitting position by the murderer. Gary then almost tripped over something, and when he looked on the floor, he saw something dark on the bare stone floor. He shone his torch on it – and saw it was a dog. Gary knew most breeds of dog and he could see that this was a black glossy coated Aberdeen terrier – and like the naked woman, it was also rigid and lifeless. Ian nudged the inert canine with his shoe and then looked at Gary. 'What the hell's going on?'

'Are they stuffed?' Gary said, and he and his colleague looked back at the nude insensible and apparently dead woman. At this point there was an ear-piercing scream in the rooms upstairs, followed by heavy thumps. The two policemen bravely went upstairs and looked into four different rooms, but could find no one. All of the décor of this house looked very old fashioned, and in the toilet, Ian found a feeble flame from some sort of gas lamp flickering on the wall. Feeling very uneasy and quite perplexed at the 'stuffed' woman and dog, the policemen went back to their car and radioed in a report which was received by the bemused radio operator. Then, as Gary was giving further details about the exact location of number 35 Grove Street as well as further information on the position of the woman in the kitchen, Ian tapped him on his shoulder.

'What?' Gary said, turning towards his partner.

Ian swore and said, 'Look, it's gone mate. Gone.'

The house they had just explored was nowhere to be seen. Not a trace of it remained. Just grass blowing in the wind where the two storey dwelling had stood moments before. Now the policemen had some explaining to do, and they tried to tell the operator what had happened, but she treated it as a joke and probably thought they were winding her up. For the next few months, Ian and Gary would purposely drive along Grove Street in the hope of once again seeing the house where they had come upon a dead woman's body sitting at a kitchen table with an apparently stuffed terrier at her feet. The policemen never saw that mirage of a house again, and to this day the extraordinary incident continues to baffle them. Was it a timeslip, or was it the grisly re-enactment of a murder from long ago being replayed or commemorated by some dark power with a gruesome sense of humour? I have scoured miles of microfilmed street directories and censuses and newspaper archives, and found no psychopathic taxidermist at large at 35 Grove Street, but the two policemen are certain what they saw, and the reports of a domestic coming from the phantom house that night also vindicates their testimony, but I think it'll be a long time before we can explain the sinister events of that night in the 1970s.

WHEN JESUS CALLS

In the latter weeks of 2012 I started looking into a rather bizarre mystery that was unfolding across Liverpool and Merseyside. People from all walks of life were hearing knocks on their doors, all hours in the morning, and quite a few of these citizens had gone to their bedroom windows or tip-toed to front door wide-angled viewers to see who was calling at such an unearthly hour, only to catch a glimpse of a man who looked like the archetypal image of Jesus, with long hair, beard and moustache, and long, quaint-looking robes. The only difference was the colouring of the night-caller's attire; most of the witnesses say he the figure dressed in grey and white, quite unlike the scarlet and white robes portrayed in statues and paintings of Christ. Is a practical joker with insomnia at work? Well, he's going to a lot of trouble if he's merely out to wind-up the locals, but of course, a prankster can never be ruled out in these cases. In one night alone

(Tuesday 11 December 2012), the mysterious robed visitant called at five addresses at Hunts Cross, Aintree, Garston, Speke and Norris Green. On each of these occasions he was seen walking away into the night, and although one person – a woman in her sixties – shouted after him, he did not react and soon left the street, leaving bare foot prints behind on the rain-slicked pavement. At the time of writing there have been sixteen reports, and nine of these seem to be centred around the Knotty Ash and Old Swan areas. A person who investigates local Fortean phenomena has informed me that there have been similar nocturnal house-calls made in Wirral, from Wallasey to Willaston. In November 2012, a family living on Wallasey's Mount Road were rudely awakened by five loud knocks on their front door at 4am, and Robert, the father of the family, went to the front door and looked through the frosted glass window to see a long-haired man with a bearded face standing there. He asked the visitor who he was and received no reply. The unknown caller then left and Robert and his family watched in disbelief from the parlour window as they saw the man walk away, because he was dressed in long robes and looked like the iconic image of Jesus Christ. The family had suffered a bereavement the week before and Robert feels as if the visit was of some religious significance; perhaps a sign that Jesus is around to ease their loss.

I felt as if I had heard of something similar to this before, and so I spent days going through my files, and discovered a letter sent to me in 2002 from a Fazakerley woman named Joan. Joan recalled how, one night in the winter of 1966, when she was ten, she overheard her mother and Gran and the next-door neighbour Mrs Fisher, talking in hushed voices around the kitchen table about someone who was knocking on doors in the middle of the night across the Walton neighbourhood. People who had answered the door were startled to see a figure who looked like Jesus standing there, and some fainted when they saw him and others experienced an amazing feeling of peace. A woman in Woolhope Road who had lost her baby had received a visit from "Our Lord" and she had been lifted out of her depression by the visitation, even though she couldn't remember much about it. When Joan asked if Jesus had visited her own house, her mother said: 'Oi! Get to bed, earwig!' And for years, Joan wondered about the strange incidents she'd heard her mum and Gran talking about.

A postman named Ian told me how, on the morning of Sunday 23 December 2012, at 3.40 am, he was staying over at his mother's house on Thingwall Lane, Knotty Ash, because his father was ill, when he and the household were roused from their sleep by five knocks on the front door. The bell is never rung in these incidents, I have noticed, and the loud knocks startled Ian, as he had to sleep on the ground floor room of his mother's house, close to the front door, and being a light sleeper, he was up within seconds and went to the window immediately. There were five other people, all relatives, staying at the house, and three of them also went to the window to see who had knocked so heavily at such an unearthly hour.

Ian saw a man about 5ft 9 in height, aged perhaps about 35, with long black hair way past his shoulders, standing on the doorstep with his back to him. He wore a long robe which looked black and grey, and the man was barefooted. Ian opened the window of the room and shouted, 'Hey!' but the man walked off. The gate was already open and the man walked through the gateway and down Thingwall Lane. Out of curiosity, Ian put on his slippers, slid the bolt off the front door and dashed outside, but the weirdly-dressed caller was nowhere to be seen. On the following morning – which was Christmas Eve, Ian's 77-year-old father, who had been suffering from flu-like symptoms which threatened to turn into pneumonia, made a rather quick recovery from his illness and asked for something to eat and drink when he awoke. No one had told him about the strange caller, but Ian's Dad said he had dreamed a glowing warm light had come into his bedroom during the night, and he felt so happy and comfortable in its presence. This could, of course, all be down to coincidence. I have noticed that in hard times of adversity, in economic recessions and in times of need, reports of angels seem to proliferate, and these 'Jesus visits' could merely be a type of urban legend generated by wishful thinking, and yet something tells me that this isn't so; perhaps *you* may even receive a call…

WILLIAM

'No Milk Today' said the note curled up in the pint bottle on Maureen Kershaw's doorstep. Jim, Maureen's husband of fifteen years had recently died from a long illness, and now Maureen felt as if she couldn't face the world – even the milkman who always asked how Jim was. She was only in her early forties but Maureen felt her life was over after losing what we would today call a 'soulmate'. Jim and her had been so close, they'd almost been telepathic, and liked the same things in life, same music, same food, same telly programmes, and now he was gone. Surely if there was a life after this, Jim would have been in touch? Maureen mused upon this each day, and longed for some sign from the world beyond – some subtle indication from the promised life beyond the grave. Nothing.

And then Maureen's old aunt, Lizzie, passed away that arctic winter in 1963, and the old woman left her favourite niece a three storey house on Canning Street. Maureen eagerly left her home in Huyton and moved in to the new residence to forget the life she'd had with Jim. However, Maureen had barely been in the new home for three days when she made a shocking discovery. A ghost was at large in the house The creepy revelation took place as Maureen was gazing out the window, wallowing in self-pity one snowy afternoon when a musical voice below said, 'Polka dot drawers! How novel my dear!'

Maureen yelped, then looked down at the floor, and she saw a man's head with wavy golden hair gazing up her skirt as he howled with laughter. For a moment, Maureen thought some burglar had tunnelled up into the living room from the cellar, but then the intruder – who was visible as far down as his shoulders – flitted into the carpeted floor and vanished. Maureen crouched down in shock, unable to understand why there wasn't a hole in the floor where the peeping Tom had been looking up her dress at her knickers. There was just smooth red carpet at that spot. Maureen felt ill with fear, and left the house to go next door to her new neighbour, old Mrs Berry. 'You'd better get used to these things because your house is haunted,' she calmly told Maureen, 'and it was like that before your auntie lived there. I couldn't tell you who the ghost is though. All these old houses have these shadows in them; they're that old, so it's to be expected I suppose. I get a smell of lavender now and then from something passing through here.'

Maureen contacted a young priest and he put her

in touch with a retired priest who had secretly studied the occult for many years, and this old former priest recommended a man named Roger Newton, a layman who had quite a reputation for exorcisms and the laying of ghosts. Roger was recovering from flu though, and said he'd visit the Canning Street house as soon as he was well enough. In the meantime the blond-haired ghost would tickle Maureen's toes as she lay in bed, and he'd kiss her on the cheek (whilst he was invisible) whenever she went out. When Maureen would play her records, a chair would dance around the room, or the ghost would appear in a mirror, dressed in outdated clothes, miming the words to the songs. On one occasion, the mischievous attention-seeking spectre pulled the cloth from the tabletop straight across the room as Maureen was eating her dinner, leaving the plates, cups, bowls and condiments all in place. Then there came laughter from the upper reaches of the chimney.

The spooky shenanigans terrified Maureen at first, but surprisingly, she soon became used to the ghost, and in a weird way, it provided the widow with some much-needed company. The blond phantom began to manifest regularly and even struck up a conversation one evening as a blizzard raged outside. 'My name is William,' the ghost announced, 'and I died after a fit of laughter in this house a long time ago,' he added.

Maureen asked him about the afterlife, but William shrugged and said, 'A lot of them over there are asleep, and some have gone to a lovely place, all sunny and sweet, but I have only glimpsed it. I come back here because I loved this house; it holds so many happy memories. Some of us come back here when we reminisce. Sentimentality I suppose.'

Maureen told William about the loss of her husband and asked if he would be able to go and see if he was 'over there' in the life beyond, but William looked down at the floor and told her it was unlikely he'd be able to find him. The next world was such a big place, and he didn't really have much to do with it. 'I'm sorry you are lonely,' he told Maureen. 'On my soul I know what loneliness is. I have walked the rooms of this house, and sometimes the streets outside, in the moonlight, when the living are asleep, and I have visited the places where I courted long ago.'

William often played the piano, even when the lid was down, and he would recite beautiful poetry with so much feeling, he would sometimes shed a tear, and he also told wonderful stories of lost loves from a bygone era. In particular he missed a lady he had once loved from afar named Lucinda, and sometimes visited her tomb in a local churchyard. Other spirits had told William that Lucinda had not gone into the world of spirit when her life ended, but lay in a type of sleep in her tomb for some reason. Some said she refused to cut the earthly ties with this world because she had been waiting for her love to join her, but that man was untrue, so now she prefers the eternal sleep of death where her heart can never be broken.

When the exorcist, Roger Newton called, Maureen sent him away. Then a second ghost – a

Mr Alfred Wiles – began to appear, and a phantom dog also. Then over the course of a few months, the house would occasionally revert back to its Victorian state, with sumptuous and elaborate furnishings of long ago. The sounds of horse's hooves and trundling carriages would be heard in the vicinity of the house, as if the past was seeping into the present. As lovely as this seemed, Maureen felt as if some unspoken law was being violated.

One summer evening that year, an old man dressed like a Quaker appeared in the hallway of the house on Canning Street, and in a rather nonchalant manner, informed Maureen he was a spirit guide. He said he had come to take the ghosts back to the hereafter, where they were supposed to be. He then went upstairs and vanished. When William and his friend Alfred appeared sometime later in the parlour, Maureen warned them about the spirit guide and advised them to make themselves scarce and lay low for a while, but the door to the parlour flew open as she spoke, and there stood the guide, and behind him was a golden light as bright as the morning sun. Maureen shielded her eyes from its intensity, and she could hear voices shouting, the barking of the spirit dog and someone crying, and it sounded like William sobbing. He begged the guide to let him stay with Maureen but then the light vanished in an instant, and so did the tumult of voices. A sweet smell like lavender hung in the air, but faded within minutes.

Maureen waited and waited for the return of her friend from beyond, but as far as I know, she never saw him again during her life on earth. She eventually mingled with the living again, and met a lovely man named Phillip. Maureen began to date Phillip, and after a courtship of just over a year she became engaged to him, and eventually married him. Maureen never forgot William, and often dreamed of him and his friend Alfred, and the little dog; three souls who brought comfort into the life of a woman who used to be so lonely and forlorn.

MAMMON

One rainy night in the 1950s, a petty 24-year-old criminal named Stan broke into a rather grand-looking building on Chatham Street, just off Myrtle Street, on the eastern periphery of Liverpool's city centre. The building had once been the Welsh Presbyterian Chapel, and had been in use from 1861 to 1949, when it was purchased by Liverpool University to house exam rooms. The front door lock to this imposing old building was one which most able burglars could pick within the minute, but Stan took a quarter of an hour, and it was almost one in the morning by the time he gained entry, but the promise of typewriters rumoured to be stored on the premises spurred him on. He hadn't been in the place long when he was forced to blow out his candle because of a great tumult of approaching footsteps outside the front door. Stan hid under a table, crouched almost in the foetal position as the lights went on and seven smartly-dressed men came into the place. Surely, they didn't hold night-classes this late? Stan thought, and he watched as one of the well turned-out strangers bolted the front door of the building. Tables and chairs were cleared at the end of the room, and in the space created, the seven men stood in a circle. One of them then left the circle to switch off the lights, and this man returned with a type of lantern. By the light of this lantern the men bowed their heads and began to chant words the amateur burglar had never heard. And suddenly, there appeared in the centre of the circle a bizarre and eerie-looking figure, reminiscent of the Buddha, only with a pair of horns. It looked like a statue at first – a pot-bellied gold idol of some sort – but then it began to speak in a deep rich echoing voice. It sounded as if it was saying, 'My disciples – you have summoned me!' And Stan squinted, scared, yet mesmerised by the golden entity, and he saw four shimmering glyphs of light appear over the unearthly being's head. Stan later sketched those glyphs for me – and I discovered that they spell the word "Mammon" in an ancient Hebrew script. Mammon is the Aramaic name of a mysterious god of money and greed mentioned in the Bible. The men standing round the demonic figure were seen to post pieces of paper into a slot in the horned head of "Mammon" and then the figures moved in and appeared to kiss and suckle the bestial manifestation. Stan bolted from his hiding place, fell over a chair, but somehow managed to get to the door. He drew back the bolt, and ran off through a heavy downpour to his home in Toxteth. Had the seven men been worshippers of Mammon? Businessmen who owed their success to the secular god of materialism? Well, its odd how, in 1864, 73-year-old Welshman Edward Price, a respected pillar of the community and a long-term member of the Welsh Presbytery, was visited in the dead of night by six men who called at his home at 73 Hanover Street. The men asked Price to join their 'sect' – a dissenting clique that now worshipped Mammon. The sect worshipped at the Welsh Chapel on Chatham Street for now but hoped to build a proper place of worship soon. The leader of the six men – a man surnamed Argent - proposed that the time had come for a religion based on the materialistic world, upon money, and economics. This religion would have a Machiavellian credo that would unashamedly advocate any political means necessary to strengthen the wealth of the nation, and the Tabernacle would be forthwith regarded as a bank vault! Glassy-eyed Argent seemed almost possessed as he continued to reveal the full scope of his sickening philosophical doctrine. Enormous workhouses for the poor would be created to harness the power of gargantuan treadmills to power up factories, and an elite class of super-wealthy industrialists would become the new aristocracy. The "Mammonite Movement" would spread throughout Europe and supersede the British Empire. Price was so shocked at these obscene proposals he collapsed and when he came to, the six men had gone. On the following morning, which happened to be a Sunday, Price told the Reverend Joshua Davies at the Chatham Street

Chapel about the "six devils" who were all members of the congregation, but those six men were nowhere to be seen. That morning, as the Reverend Davies recited a sermon he had edited to include a message about the dangers of putting profit before belief, he quoted extracts from the Gospels of Matthew and Luke which mentioned Mammon, who he termed "the devil of covetousness" and in the midst of the sermon, Henry Price cried out and slumped onto the bench. He had died of a massive heart attack.

A young reporter from the *Liverpool Courier* named John Weightman later heard about the strange scandalous sect of Mammonites and set out to investigate and expose them, but soon found that the cult had many friends in very high places, and several prominent and influential people, including magistrates, wealthy businessmen, and two Members of Parliament were rumoured to be members of the clandestine extremist sect. Weightman received letters detailing anonymous death threats which he dismissed at first, but one foggy evening as he was returning to his home on Hope Place, a shadowy caped man approached him and aimed a pistol at his head. The stranger told the journalist to discontinue his delving into matters which should not concern him. 'There will not be a second warning,' the man then said, and after putting the pistol away, he casually walked off into the fog. Weightman reluctantly decided not to pursue his investigations any further.

Whether or not the followers of Mammon succeeded in their quest for global domination is unknown, but some would probably say that Capitalism has beaten them to it. In one respect, Mammon might have triumphed in that former Welsh Presbyterian Chapel on Chatham Street, because today, in a place where the faithful once worshipped God, people of a secular, materialistic belief congregate, for the former chapel is now the University of Liverpool Management School.

THE MAD WIDOW

The locals called Toxteth's Mann Street "Murder Street" back in Victorian times, for so many killings took place there over the years, the most shocking being the murder of Mary Jane McNamara by Robert Black in 1884. Black smashed an oil lamp into Mary Jane's Face and watched callously as she became a human torch. The street was also a rife with suicide, and the year of the McNamara murder – 1884 – a very sinister 'suicide' took place in Mann Street. Hannah Armstrong was 52 but looked twenty years younger. She had glossy raven black hair tied up neatly in a bun, and was married to a man who worked at a local foundry as a striker. Hannah bumped into an old acquaintance one day in September of that year as she shopped on Bold

Street, and it seems that this old friend, a lady named Philomena, informed Hannah that a man she had been very fond of many years ago had recently died from influenza. Hannah was heartbroken by the news and went into a depression, known in those times as melancholia and low spirits. Hannah took to wearing a mantilla lace of the sort worn by widows, and this naturally caused her husband to question her sanity. Hannah would walk her neighbourhood in her black lace veil and funereal attire, much to the amusement of the children of the streets, especially when the "widow" began to pull tongues at the mocking children. Mr Armstrong seems to have attempted to have his wife committed to an asylum, but was unsuccessful, for the family doctor said the strange behaviour of Hannah would soon pass, but it only became more bizarre. Hannah would peep out from behind the lace curtains of the bay window of her parlour and pull tongues at children, and one morning two sisters – aged seven and eight - from nearby Hill Street were passing the house at 152 Mann Street when they saw the madcap woman shaking violently as she pulled an enormous tongue at them from behind the drapes. The girls giggled and ran off to tell their mother of the tongue-pulling incident. 'Keep away from that house,' their mother warned, 'That poor lady is insane.'

Later that morning, a boy peered into the parlour and saw Hannah Armstrong dead on the floor. She had been strangled, and her tongue was swollen and hanging limp from her mouth. The coroner Clarke Aspinall said Hannah had strangled herself, but other medical experts disagreed, saying such a thing was impossible, because a person would automatically let go of the throat as a reflex action before asphyxia could occur, but self-strangulation remained the official cause of death. There were rumours that a sinister strangler had stood behind the curtain, throttling Hannah as the two little girls from Hill Street had looked on, unaware of what was happening. Not long afterwards, the solid-looking ghost of Hannah was seen prowling the streets of Toxteth, pulling tongues and shaking her veiled head violently as if invisible hands were gripping her throat. It was said that all who saw her suffered terrible misfortune, and for many months while the ghost walked the neighbourhood after dusk, people would stay off the streets and draw their curtains, because the "Mad Widow" had a creepy habit of peering through windows. The ghost went into hibernation for many years, then began to walk again in the 1930s. She was also allegedly seen as recently as January 2002 walking along Park Road one frosty moonlit morning at 1.30am. When the apparition of the woman in black reached the Globe pub, it suddenly vanished. A taxi driver named Malcolm who has now retired tells me that in 1996 he almost hit a woman in outdated black clothes near the Toxteth Tabernacle on Park Road around 11 o'clock at night, and he stopped, and reversed to give the oddball jaywalker a piece of his mind, but when he saw the woman's chalk white face behind the dark veil, along with her weird staring eyes, he quickly drove off. On the following morning, Malcolm's brother died of a massive heart attack while visiting him, and the cabby believes the woman in black he had a close shave with the night before the death was some omen.

HALEWOOD'S OLD HAG

In 1972, a 21-year-old veterinary student named Cecilia met a trainee doctor named Lewis at the YMCA on Mount Pleasant, and within months of their first date, they moved into a draughty old flat on Catharine Street. Everyone said Cecilia and Lewis made such a lovely couple, and when Cecilia became pregnant, Lewis proposed in the Philharmonic pub, Cecilia accepted, and an engagement ring was produced. Wedding bells were soon going to chime, and Cecilia's friend Carol said she envied her, as she had wanted to marry and settle down to start a family ever since she was seventeen. 'It's not Lewis's baby,' Cecilia suddenly told Carol at the latter's flat on Bold Place. Carol's jaw dropped, she thinned her eyes in disbelief.

'Yeah, it's not his,' Cecilia reaffirmed the shocking sordid truth, and began to cry. She hugged Carol and the unpalatable facts of the matter came out. It had happened when Lewis had been away for a month on a training course in Carlisle. Cecilia had met a young black physical education teacher named Carl at the university gymnasium, and he had invited her to a party at a house in Halewood. She became drunk and went into a bedroom with Carl and they made love. It had just been pure physical attraction, nothing more. Carl was already married and in the morning Cecilia had awakened alone. She felt sick and cheap when she realised what she had done. She loved only one man in this world, and that was Lewis, and now she felt so ashamed of her mindless one night stand, and knew she'd lose her love if she told him the baby wasn't his.

'But you've got to tell him,' Carol advised, 'he'll know as soon as he sees the baby isn't white.'

Cecilia shook her head. 'I can't tell him, and I can't get rid of my baby, I felt him kick for the first time the other day. I just know it's a boy.'

'What are you going to do?' Carol clutched her friend's hands tightly.

'Lewis has told everyone he's going to be a dad; he's so proud – ' Cecilia's voice trailed off into choking sobs, and Carol embraced her and felt powerless to give any sound advice.

All of the stress from carrying so much guilt proved too much for Cecilia, and a week before she was due to go into the maternity hospital, she decided to leave Lewis. She sneaked out of the flat one morning, and didn't even leave a note explaining the dramatic departure. Cecilia went to see her Aunt Claudia in Halewood, and explained to her aunt why she'd come to see her. Claudia said the main thing at the moment was for Cecilia to rest, for her own sake and the baby's too.

That night, Cecilia fell asleep in the single bed in the spare room. It's a strange thing, but most people can never remember the exact point when a dream begins. If we are awakened while having a nightmare, we usually recall the point where we wake up and the nightmare ends, but whom among us can recall exactly when a dream begins? Cecilia recalled having some strange dreams that night, and this was to be expected, because of all of the stress and worry her mind had been subjected to of late, but throughout the odd dreams of shadowy figures and weird music, Cecilia could smell something ghastly; the odour reminded her of milk that had gone off, only more potent. Cecilia was awakened around 3.40 am by something. She opened her eyes and found the room partially illuminated by a street lamp shining its weak amber light through the net curtains. Cecilia suddenly felt as if someone wa sitting on her shins. Someone was on her bed, moving about! Cecilia reached out to turn on the bedside lamp, but was suddenly struck with paralysis.

A hand in a black tight-fitting glove reached out towards her face. The fingers were unnaturally long and thin - and then a grotesque, terrifying face swum into view. It was a heavily wrinkled face with bulging eyes encircled by dark rings. The breath of this woman - who wore a black hood - was rancid, and Cecilia immediately recognised the stomach-churning odour as the one she had been catching a whiff of in her troubled dreams.

'I'll have that baby of yours!' the eerie old woman in black screeched, and her bony fingers felt

Cecilia's hump and began to scratch at it through the blankets, as if it intended to claw out the unborn child.

Cecilia managed to let out a scream, and she saw the woman run off the bed and onto the floor on all fours like a spider as her thin arms and legs moved with lightning agility. The entity seemed to flee towards a dark corner of the room. The unearthly old hag then returned to the bed and once again sat on Cecilia's legs, only this time she gazed at the door with her head tilted, listening to the approach of Aunt Claudia, who had been startled from her slumbers by her niece's scream.

Aunt Claudia burst into the room, and for a moment she saw the bizarre woman dressed in a tight-fitting black costume and pointed long shoes sitting on the bed. And then the freak was gone; she was there one moment, gone the next, and when she vanished into thin air, Cecilia felt the woman's meagre weight lift from her legs.

'Oh my God!' exclaimed Claudia, and she threw her hands up to her face as she recalled the ghastly shrivelled face of the bedroom intruder. She looked at the spot on the bed where the monstrosity had sat a few seconds ago, fearful that it would reappear.

Cecilia went into labour with fright and Claudia had to leave the house to call an ambulance from a telephone box. Cecilia was admitted to hospital, and Claudia telephoned Lewis to tell him what had happened. Claudia also broke the truth to Lewis about the baby not being his.

On the following morning at 10am, Lewis sat with Cecilia as she began to have the baby. She was in great pain and kept apologising to Lewis and telling him she was sorry for what she had done.

Lewis told her over and over that he loved her more than anything in the world. Later that morning, Cecilia gave birth to a boy, and on the baby's back there was a clot of blood shaped exactly like a long-fingered hand. Cecilia screamed when she saw the mark, because it looked exactly like the hand of the old hag that had appeared on her bed last night and scratched at her tummy. The nurses present said the mark was just a stain, and one of them wiped it off, although one of the nurses did say the stain looked remarkably like a hand, and it was much longer than the midwife's hand, so it could not have been an imprint made through transferral of blood.

Lewis later accepted the baby as if it was his own, and forgave Cecilia for her 'lapse' as he called it. The couple are still together today and have quite a large family now.

The house in Halewood where the sinister black clad old woman pounced on the pregnant Cecilia is but a stone's throw from a row of streets where a number of "Old Hag" attacks took place in the 1990s. Old Hag Syndrome has been covered before in my books and columns and concerns a widely-reported phenomenon whereby a person awakes in his or her bed and finds they are unable to move. During this alarming paralysis, the person often senses there is someone or something malevolent in the room, and on most occasions the presence is indicated by the detection of a bad smell. The paralysed person then often feels this presence climb onto the bed, but on some occasions the person awakes in a state of paralysis to feel something pressing down on the chest area. Many of the reports are of a woman in dark or black clothes who has a wrinkled ugly wizened face, hence the name of this syndrome – Old Hag.

The intriguing thing about some of these Old Hag attacks is the way they are often reported in clusters, often stretching across rows of houses and streets. If the attacks happened to just one person, it could probably be explained as nothing more than a nightmare that has spilled over into waking reality for a short while, but in the Halewood cases I researched some years ago, the Old Hag terrorised over six people living in neighbouring streets. Some instances of sleep paralysis are similar to Old Hag Syndrome, but are usually caused by more mundane reasons (stress, over-tiredness, sleeping on the back, etc) but the Hag has been reported for centuries and seems to be a form of succubus (a demonic female who preys on both men and women). The Hag will often appear in a house which has no history of hauntings, although I discovered that in the case of the incident at Halewood concerning Cecilia, a ouija board had been used in the spare room in 1951 by a friend of Claudia. This might have had some bearing on the reasons behind the chilling nocturnal visit.

IN A VISION ONCE I SAW

The following stories were related to me by readers at several booksignings. The first one dovetails with the second one because they both concern incidents that happened in the same area and involve very similar phenomena.

In the summer of 1982 in the middle of one of the worst recessions to ever hit Britain, three million people were unemployed, and two of these forsaken souls were brothers named Rhys (aged 27) and David (aged 22) and they came from the Aintree area of Liverpool. In the wasteland of Thatcher's Britain, there seemed to be no light at the end of the tunnel, and both men were forever being sent on pointless courses and 'Job Restarts'. In the summer of despair, Rhys seemed to be edging close to a nervous breakdown. He began to lose interest in football, his guitar, and even in the opposite sex. He began to ramble over breakfast each morning about emigrating to Australia and the United States, and of a revolution that would surely come when people refused to be pushed around by the lying

Government anymore. The father of the family would always say things were not as bad as the Depression he had lived through in the 1930s, and Rhys would say, 'Yeah, that's all in the past, Dad, this is different.'

And the father of the family would always smile and shake his head and say: 'They need a world war. This crap has gone on too long, it's stagnant; the music today, the telly, everything, it's shite. We've had fifty years of shite and now it can't go any further. The Russians will kick off soon, and that's when the fun will start. A lovely big war to get rid of all the dead wood.'

'Oh shut up you stupid old dickhead! You've got a screw loose wanting everyone dead!' Rhys would yell and run up to his room.

And on this day, that was exactly how the script went. Father sitting in the kitchen with morning TV turned down low in the background, dreaming of a world war to shake up the world he couldn't take to as he rolled another carcinogenic cigarette. The timid mother of the boys would continually be brewing pot after pot of tea to top up the discursive Dad as he coughed and wheezed through his strange militaristic philosophy.

Rhys finally snapped and left the low-ceilinged kitchen and went up to his room to pack. David went up after him and asked if he could borrow his Hondo acoustic guitar.

Rhys nodded and then told his brother: 'Keep it if you like.'

David knew something was wrong when Rhys said something like that. 'Nah, I just want to practise a few bar chords.'

'Keep it,' Rhys reiterated.

'Why are you packing?' David asked, placing the Hondo on its stand in the corner.

'I've had enough of the 'arl fellah. I'm going to see an old mate from school up at Pygon's Hill. He's got a farm,' Rhys replied, pressing two tee shirts into the suitcase.

'A Farm?' David immediately fell in love with the idea of working on a farm. 'Where's Pygon's Hill?'

'Up by Lydiate,' Rhys told his brother, then halted packing for a moment and said, 'And don't tell me you don't know where Lydiate is.'

'Up north,' David replied sulkily, 'I'm not that stupid.'

'Are you coming with me or staying here?' Rhys wanted to know.

'Coming with you of course,' David replied eagerly. 'What bus goes up to Pygon's Hill?'

'Am walking. I'm skint,' said Rhys, and then as he pressed the suitcase shut he asked: 'Have you got any money on you?'

David shook his head. The young man never deluded himself into thinking he was in shape. He knew he was overweight and out of shape, whereas Rhys ran a few miles almost every day and always seemed to be training for some half-marathon.

'You won't be able to walk as far as Lydiate,' Rhys said in an irritating dismissive and condescending manner, then went to comb his hair in the bathroom mirror. David followed him saying 'I'll be okay, I'm not *that* out of shape.'

Within half an hour they'd left the house slyly via

the backyard door, so as not to be seen by the totalitarian father. He'd ask too many questions and try his utmost to put his sons off trying to find work on a farm. He'd rather have them joining the army.

The brothers had only got four hundred yards from the house when they bumped into their older sister Monica. She'd been on her way to work at the Victoria Wine off-licence, and asked the lads where they were going. 'Going to try and get a job on a farm up near Lydiate,' Rhys had said, avoiding eye contact with his sister.

Monica seemed stuck for words and wore a worried look.

'I've had me dad up to here,' Rhys looked as if he was giving a salute with his index finger parallel to his eyebrow. 'He's going worse.'

'Do you want to stay in my place?' Monica asked Rhys, and then she glanced at David and asked, 'Are you going with him?' David smirked and nodded.

'Oh don't be daft, come and stay in my place for a while,' Monica suggested, and she went to get the keys of her flat out of her purse, but Rhys shook his head and walked on. 'I should be married now and settling down in my own place instead of being stuck with my mum and dad, it's pathetic,' he told his sympathetic sister.

Monica shouted something after her brothers but they walked on through the August sunshine.

Three times during the northward trek, Rhys threatened to leave his brother behind. David would come to a gasping halt every mile or so and say he just needed a rest, and Rhys would curse and swear and lament about people holding him back, and then after a minute of moaning he'd pat a tearful David on the back and wait until his unfit brother regained his breath and stamina.

The desperate duo reached Bell's Lane, which was just a dirt track in the middle of a shimmering field near Maghull, when Rhys finally admitted he had lost his bearings. They were going west instead of north, he realised, and at this point in the odyssey to find work, something very strange took place. The lads walked through thick thigh-length grass and weeds bordering a field of barley. 'God, it's like *Bellamy's Backyard Safari* here. Let's go back and go down that other road,' said Rhys, and then he began to rant about being unemployable and how better things would be in Australia, when suddenly, David pointed at something in the distance and said, 'Hey, look at that!'

Rhys stopped grumbling and looked up to the horizon. 'What the fu – '

Across the fields, about a mile and a half beyond two misted National Grid pylons, there was a beautiful, mysterious spectacle: an exotic city of silvery blue. It had not been there seconds ago and its sudden appearance scared David. The only frame or reference in David's mind was the Indo-Saracenic buildings he had seen as a child on a day-trip to Brighton, and vague recollections of the pictures of he Taj Mahal he had seen in his schoolbooks. He and Rhys beheld the hazed blue pagodas, towers, minarets, and onion-bulb domes. It was like some desert metropolis out of the Arabian Nights – but how? Shouldn't Sefton be there instead?

Rhys swore and then he kept saying 'Where is it? Where is it?'

And all the time he was hurrying towards this mirage.

'Don't go over there Rhys,' David advised, and as he squinted at the vision, he thought he could even see tiny figures moving up in a speeded-up fashion, like the people in the old Charlie Chaplin films.

'Can you see people running dead fast across some sort of gardens?' Rhys asked his frightened brother.

'Yeah, hang on, don't go over there,' David tried to pull his spellbound brother back by his forearm but Rhys began to trot across the field towards the eerie city, which now seemed to rise and fall and undulate as if it was resting on a cushion of hot air. It was like the phantom illusory pools of non-existent water you saw on motorways on such scorching days as this.

Then the silvery city magnified slightly. It expanded as if it was made of liquid mercury – as if the eastern domes were made of quicksilver, and the sudden magnification created the unsettling illusion of the field being in motion. The field of barley the brothers were trespassing upon seemed to be moving south, but then the optical illusion ended when the city reverted back to its original size. Rhys still kept hurrying towards it, and David soon found himself out of breath on such an infernal day. He tried to shout out a warning to his curious brother but his voice died in his parched throat. He was bent over, hands above each knee, gasping for air with a stitch in his side.

David looked up and saw Rhys racing across the field. He watched him until he was just a spot in the distance, and then that spot and the ominous shimmering city vanished. The pylons were visible again, and beyond them, parts of Sefton. David walked and walked and searched for his brother, but he was nowhere to be seen. He tread through hardened clods of soil on farmland and saw no one for miles. He ended up near Sefton Meadows and here he met a girl, the daughter of a farmer, and told her what had happened. The mention of the mirage made her eyes widen and she gave David the impression she had either seen that mirage herself in the past or had heard about it before from someone. The girl advised the young man from Aintree to inform the police, and this is what David did. A week went by, and no one could find Rhys. All of the relatives of the family came together and searched Lydiate and Maghull for Rhys, and it soon became clear that no one in these areas had seen him. And then, exactly a week after Rhys vanished, he turned up in a terrible state at his home in Aintree. His face was unshaven and dirty, and his tee shirt had been ripped at the side with the tear going up to his left armpit. He had no trainers on, and he sported a black eye. For days he said nothing, and appeared to be terrified of something. He tried to hide in the cubby hole under the stairs in his home, and burst into tears when the family doctor came out to have a look at him. The doctor was of the opinion that Rhys had suffered a nervous breakdown, and within days he was transferred to hospital, where he was kept in for observation for several weeks. In the following month, Rhys's behaviour returned to normal, and he could not remember what had happened after he had run towards that mirage. Years later, hypnosis was tried, but all Rhys could see was an impenetrable blackness when he was in a trance, and a strange silence would fill his ears. The brothers never again ventured anywhere near Bell's Lane in Lydiate in case the 'eastern' city returned.

When this case was first reported to me by David, I immediately thought of another case of a mirage incident, and this was in the very same area around Lydiate and Sefton. I feel this other incident is certainly connected to the 1982 case. The story came my way from a reader of my work at a booksigning event at Borders in Birkenhead a few years back. The woman who told the story to me was in her eighties but very lucid and blessed with a good memory. Her name was Elizabeth, and she told me the story as she recalled it from her mother, a very strict and religious woman who was not prone to flights of fancy; she certainly held no belief in ghosts.

In 1914, a group of children from Sefton village rushed up to a policeman one beautifully sunny afternoon and told him that they had seen something very strange out on Sefton Meadows. At the time, the meadows – which had always been prone to flooding because of their flatness – were like swamps, and the police constable told the children to keep away from the area because a young boy had almost been sucked under the quagmire of mud in the meadows a few weeks back.

The children excitedly urged the officer of the law to go and see the 'thing' which had appeared on Sefton Meadows, and the oldest child among the group – a 12-year-old girl named Sue, who was known for being a very honest and responsible person, assured the constable that a town had appeared on the edge of the meadows.

'Its probably the circus,' the policeman laughed, 'is it a tent like? Is that what you've all seen?'

'No, sir,' Sue shook her head, 'please come and see for yourself.'

The policeman therefore went off with the children leading the way, and as he neared Sefton Meadows, he saw to his utter astonishment, that there was indeed a very strange town visible to the north, about two miles away, and the River Alt was running into it. The buildings of the town looked as if they were metallic, and the architecture was weird. The policeman could see four spires taller than any he had seen on any local church, and they were rising up from a glittering building of silver and gold. There were also a number of domes of enormous proportions behind this building, surrounded by other smaller but equally exotic-looking buildings. A low cloud passed over the unknown town, casting its shadow upon it, and when the cloud had passed, there were only the usual fields and distant trees visible where the town had existed seconds ago. The children gasped out loud at this, then turned their little faces to the policeman as if he would have some explanation to account for the supernatural proceedings, but all the copper said was, 'Come on you lot, let's be getting home.'

'Can we go and see what it was?' asked one of the children, but the policeman, who was still staring at the scene of one of the most amazing spectacles he had ever witnessed, shook his head. He told the children they'd get into trouble if they trespassed on the farmer's land, and he had a very difficult time shepherding the hyperactive kids back to the village.

Later that year a strange rumour gained currency among the locals. A young soldier who was about to be sent to fight for his country in WWI had decided to desert, and had fled across Sefton Meadows after seeing the phantom town appear in the mists one morning. The soldier believed the scintillating buildings were some religious gateway to another world, and ran across the flooded meadows with police and army officials in pursuit. The soldier got within about 200 yards of one of the spectral buildings and saw a group of unusually tall figures dressed in bright white robes. These mysterious figures held their arms out towards the deserter, but the frightened soldier suddenly fell face down into the muddy water, and when he got up, two policemen seized him and dragged him away, and the mirage-like town had vanished into thin air. Elizabeth, who told me this story, said the deserter was later killed by a firing squad for desertion. During World War One, some 306 British and Commonwealth soldiers were executed by firing squad for cowardice and desertion, and a few of those shot to death by firing squads were just 16. A case that stands out in my memory is that of 16-year-old James Crozier from Belfast, who was shot at dawn for desertion. Before he was killed by the 12-men firing squad, he was given so much rum, he passed out and had to be dragged to the spot where he was shot. Some of the deserters were tied up from head to toe so they could not move, and they had to be carried to the place appointed for the execution. One 17-year-old saw his friend blown to bits by a shell in France, and when he saw the dismembered arms and legs and the face peppered with deep pits inflicted by the shell shrapnel, he turned and ran. He was subsequently charged with cowardice and killed by a firing squad.

The area where the mirage of the phantom town has been seen has been associated with so-called "Elf Paths" for centuries. These Elf Paths, also known as Ley Lines of Power, have allegedly been detected by dowsers and various mediums, and they are said to criss-cross Sefton, and that includes Sefton Meadows. Where there are Elf Paths, our world seems to overlap with another reality, and people in the vicinity of such paths are more likely to see UFOs, ghosts and other paranormal phenomena. Back in February 1870, dozens of people congregated upon an ice-covered Sefton Meadows to skate, and many of these skaters reported feeling electricity in the air. A strange green glow like the Northern Lights was also seen over Sefton Meadows that evening.

THE SINISTER

In May 1968, a controversial cult horror film called *Witchfinder General* – which starred Vincent Price as the sadistic and opportunistic hunter of alleged witches in 17th century England – was released, and a fourteen-year-old lad from Huyton named Glynn somehow managed to sneak into a cinema to see this violent X-rated movie. Glynn was addicted to horror films, but was a rather impressionable teenager. After he had seen a Dracula film the year before, he had decided to become a real-life Van Helsing, and went off in search of vampires armed with a wooden stake (a leg of an old chair shaved to a point), a copy of his grandmother's Bible, and a bottle of holy water he'd obtained from the font of Huyton Parish Church. And then he met 13-year-old Louise, who was obsessed with the supernatural, and in the hunting of ghosts and evil spirits in particular, and so it was a match made in heaven. The young couple went on their first date in a graveyard, stalking spectres and attempting to conjure up the dead. Very romantic. Glynn's parents were not too keen on Louise because of her fixation with Hammer horror films and her love of dark clothes. Looking back today, Louise thinks she was an early Goth.

In July 1968, Glynn's grandfather Toby, paid a visit from his home in Dovecot, and over dinner he was reminiscing about his early courtship when he happened to say something which immediately captured his grandson's macabre imagination. The comment also enraged Glynn's parents. Toby said a local woman in Woolfall Heath he once went out with was a witch. The woman, named Penelope, looked as if she was in her twenties but dressed as if she was in the 1950s. Toby was 70, and he said he had dated Penelope back when he was 25.

'That woman never ages,' Toby told a spellbound Glynn, 'and I have always had the impression she's a witch. I have never once seen her by the light of the sun.'

'A witch?' Glynn looked at his grandfather open mouthed in awe with a roastie impaled on the end of his erect fork.

Glynn's mother told Toby to stop filling her son's head with nonsense, but Glynn was hooked, and after dinner he went into the back garden were Toby was sipping a shandy as he relaxed in a deckchair, and the lad asked: 'Grand-dad, this Penelope – do you really think she was a witch?'

Toby looked around in case Glynn's parents were about, but they were on the front lawn talking to neighbours on this beautiful summer day. 'Well, she could be,' Toby whispered, and coughed. 'She has not aged one day since – let me see – 1923. I was twenty-five in 1923, and she said she was around my age but she never did tell me exactly how old she was. Some women are like that – usually older women though.'

'Why would a witch be living round here though?' Glynn wondered out loud, and he sat on an old card table next to the deckchair.

'They have to live somewhere I suppose,' Toby grinned, and sipped the bitter shandy, then threw back his silver-crowned head. He squinted as his mind snaked back through the decades to a Liverpool of long ago, He recalled the wintry moonlit evening in 1923 at a restaurant on Ranelagh Street, not far from the old Lewis's – the Lewis's that would be destroyed, like many of the buildings on that part of the street – in the May Blitz of 1941. Toby could just about remember the food and the red wine and Penelope's huge dark eyes and her hair of spun gold. He recalled the fox stole she had worn and the cute cloche hat. He used to be able to recall her voice, but in age his auditory memory had become faded, and now all he could recall were snatches of sentences she had spoken in his mind's ear. Toby did remember holding her soft white hand across the table, and making silly promises of undying love, but it had all come to nothing. Three dates, and that was it. She didn't want to see him after that. Not once had he seen Penelope, with her skin as pale as moonlight, during the hours of the day. She had to have been a witch. Dwelling on the 'what if' of it all, Toby remembered going home heartbroken on that lonely tram in its green and white livery up Brownlow Hill. He had been so depressed after that brush-off, but looking back now, Toby dismissed the emotional turmoil of his younger self with a wry smile. You cannot be wise and be in love, he silently mused.

'Do you think she has a broomstick?' Glynn burst the soap bubble of nostalgia, bringing Toby back to his arthritic existence of today.

The old man smiled and replied: 'Probably has a vacuum cleaner nowadays.'

'What?' Glynn grimaced.

Toby screwed his old face up; a Venetian blind of wrinkles formed on his forehead. 'Look, she has probably just aged well. Some people do. We are not all the same. Its like cars; some become rust buckets and end up in the scrapyard before their time and some go on for years and become vintage models.'

'But you said you thought she was a witch,' Glynn reminded the old man of his dark suspicions. 'You never talk about stuff like that – about the supernatural and that.'

Glynn managed to extract the vital information from his grandfather which he needed for the forthcoming mission. He discovered the exact address where Penelope lived in Woolfall Heath, as well as a good description of the woman. Toby had seen her from buses passing her neighbourhood a few times always after dark or on late wintry afternoons when the sun had gone down, and on one occasion, on a gloomy late January afternoon around 5.25pm, he had stood next to her in an adjacent queue in the post office and she had not recognised him – or perhaps had chosen to ignore him. She had looked exactly as she had done in the 1920s, only the cloche and fox stole had gone and she had chosen to dress in the style of the 1950s for some reason. It was Penelope, and not some daughter or relative – and that did not make any sense to Toby – unless…

That evening in his bedroom, Louise was briefed by Glynn. The girl was so excited at becoming a deputy Witchfinder General; her beautiful eyes sparkled like the Pleiades, and she held the old black leather-bound copy of her family Bible to her pounding chest. Louise prided herself in knowing the Latin version of the Lord's Prayer, and that would be used in the confrontation with the witch. Louise said it was a pity the River Alt wasn't deep enough because she and Glynn could have thrown Penelope into it.

'We won't need to,' Glynn told her, and he took out a plastic statue of the Virgin Mary filled with holy water taken from the font of St Michael's Church. 'This will be thrown in her face, and she will not be able to bear it.'

'She might dissolve,' Louise said and smirked, and saw a deflating witch from *The Wizard of Oz* in her mind's eye.

'This is serious, Louise,' Glynn reminded his girlfriend of the gravity of what lay ahead. 'God knows what this woman is into. She might have sacrificed babies for all we know.'

The couple of witch-hunters prowled Woolfall Heath after dark, but the first night was a disaster when a local gang wondered why Glynn and Louise were hanging round their patch, and gave chase. But on the second night, as a full moon rose over the rooftops of suburban Huyton, Glynn and Louise spotted their prey. Penelope got out of a long stylish black car which looked like a limousine on Cartmel Road. She waved to the silhouetted driver and then came walking towards the teens. She was thinner and taller than they imagined, and was dressed in a black fur coat, pencil skirt, black stockings and stilettos. She was as blonde and as beautiful as she had been in 1923 when Glynn's grandfather had pined for her love, and looked about 27.

'Ready?' Louise asked her boyfriend, and he nodded. He took the bottle of holy water from his coat pocket, and unscrewed the cap.'

The clacking echoing sounds of the witch's stilettos grew in intensity as she drew near.

She passed Glynn, and for a moment, Louise shot a puzzled look at him, thinking he had lost his nerve, but the boy then shouted to Penelope: 'Excuse me miss!'

The woman stopped, and turned to look at the teenager.

In that heart-stopping moment, Glynn repeatedly made swiping movements with the plastic bottle of holy water, as if he was holding the handle of an invisible sword, and with each swipe, a string of water flew out of the bottle and splashed Penelope's face, neck and hands as she thrust her palms out reflexively to protect herself. The woman paused with a look of pure shock on her face for a moment, and then she let out a bloodcurdling scream and threw her hands to her face as if she'd had acid thrown at her. Louise held the Bible out to her and recited the Lord's Prayer. There were streaks of blood on the woman's face, which physically changed before the eyes of the frightened teenagers. What had been a most attractive face touched up with delicate beige foundation was now stretching lengthways in a grotesque unearthly manner – and then the woman's mouth opened into a huge yawning hole ringed with fangs.

Louise screamed and almost dropped the Bible.

"Penelope" fell down onto all fours and ran off like some frightened animal into the shadows of Liverpool Road. A curious trail of blood and clothing items led to a field, where the teens found the woman's high heels and her fur coat. They ran to Glynn's house in terror, believing they had just confronted not a witch – but a vampire of some sort.

Penelope was never seen again, and I have checked this out and found it to be true. Glynn's parents believed their lad and his girl merely had an overactive imagination (and that's not surprising when we bear in mind the way Glynn was influenced by the horror films he was always watching), but Toby believed the young couple's story and decided to speak to the neighbours of Penelope. No one knew anything about her, and one neighbour decided to break into the missing woman's house to see if she was there. All of the windows were covered in old WWII blackout curtains and there wasn't a stick of furniture in the place – except for an old wardrobe in the room upstairs, and it was crammed with old-fashioned clothes dating back to the 1930s.

I had heard about this female vampiric entity years ago from listeners to my slots on various radio stations, and some Huytonians were of the opinion that the female vampire was still active, but had now moved to the outskirts of Widnes…

A WARNING VOICE FROM BEYOND

In 1977, a 20-year-old Litherland woman named Lily was working at a certain well-known shop on Bold Street when a man in his forties came in to buy something, and after he had purchased the item, the man, named Rory, stopped at the door on his way out, then looked back at Lily at the counter with a slight smile on his face which sent her blushing. 'You might think this is corny, but has anyone ever told you that you're absolutely beautiful?' Rory asked.

Lily felt her face burn with embarrassment, and she was stuck for words, for no one had ever uttered such a compliment at this girl. Before Lily could say 'Oh, thanks,' Rory had pulled open the shop door and the bell above that door jangled and drowned out her words of reply. Lily watched the man who had shot such a lovely and apparently genuine compliment at her walk off into grey Bold

Street, turning the collar of his coat up as he hurried through a September downpour. For the rest of that day, Lily thought about the charming man, and wondered what his name was. Would he perhaps come into the shop again? She wondered, and as business was slack, Lily went to the spot where Rory had stood when he had made the flattering remark, and she pictured how she must have looked to him from this viewpoint near the door. He'd seen her behind the counter of course, and as Lily replayed the scene of Rory suddenly reappeared. He looked through the window of the door and smiled, and Lily once again blushed and quickly opened the door to see what he wanted.

'Look, I know I'm a bit older than you,' Rory said, 'but I'd love to take you out.'

Lily felt her mouth dry up in her head and her heart palpitated. 'Oh,' she muttered.

'Are you with someone?' Rory inquired.

'No, no, I'm not,' Lily replied, and there was a pause between the two of them.

'Do you fancy going to dinner at the Adelphi tomorrow? Say around eight?' Rory proposed, and now, from closer quarters, Lily could see his eyes were of a very pale blue, and he had slight lines - crow's feet — but nice wrinkles that gave him masculine character. He was quite tall too, around an inch or two over six foot.

'Er, yeah, okay,' Lily said, and then giggled. This was all happening a bit too fast. This man was very forward.

'I'm Rory by the way,' he said tersely, and his large hairy-backed hand gripped the slender pale hand of

Lily and held it firmly. 'I can either pick you up at your home, or you can meet me at the Adelphi? Do you know where the Adelphi is?'

'I'll meet you at the Adelphi; yes I know where it is. My name's Lily,' she said, and tried to shake his hand but it was a dead weight, and hard to move. That bulky fist shook briefly and then released Lily's hand.

He told Lily he lived off Catharine Street. He said he wasn't in the habit of asking girls out after merely setting eyes on them, but in this case it seemed to be a case of love at first sight. Lily smirked at the term, but Rory read her faint scepticism and said, 'I know it sounds like a cliché but I mean it – I saw you there – ' and his eyes glanced over to the counter, 'and I just, well, I don't know really – but something happened. I thought you looked beautiful, and I walked away, but when I got to the end of the street, I felt I had to come back and ask you out. Is that nuts?'

'No, I don't suppose so,' Lily's large eyes looked at her fidgeting hands from under the heavy lids. Her long black eyelashes fluttered. She didn't know whether Rory was serious or whether there was some ulterior motive to all this sweet talk.

'Well, I'd better be going,' Rory said, turning the collar of his coat up again.

'Okay,' Lily looked up at him.

He gripped her hand, lifted it, and leaned forward to kiss her knuckle. 'Eight o'clock tomorrow then?'

'Yeah,' Lily said, and beamed a huge smile. This was like some dream. The proceedings of this rainy day had quite an air of unreality about it.

Well, Lily told her mother Kate about Rory as soon as she got home, and Kate naturally had her suspicions. 'He's too old for you, Lil,' Kate told her daughter as she did the washing up. 'Go with someone your own age. He's got a cheek asking you out, the bleeding cradle-snatcher.'

'Mum, he's lovely though, and there's something about him,' Lily said, selfishly letting her mother wash and dry every item of the crockery and cutlery as she stood leaning against the cooker with her arms folded, gazing into space.

'He's too old Lily, what do you want to go with an old fogey for?' said Kate.

'When he smiles Mum, his eyes smile and light up as well,' Lily recalled, and she began to unconsciously imitate Rory's smile.

'Oh stop it, I'm going to bring my tea back up,' Kate grimaced.

Lily then went up to her room to choose an outfit for tomorrow, and after she had chosen the skirt, top and shoes, she decided she'd have to straighten her hair. Lily had hair that curled and frizzed when just the slightest bit of moisture was present in the air, and she prayed that the rain would stay away tomorrow night.

On the following morning, Lily awoke before her alarm clock went off with a high-pitched whistling sound in her left ear. Being a hypochondriac who believed even the slightest symptom was the beginning of some fatal medical condition, Lily went into her mum's bedroom and woke her to tell her of the whistle in her ear.

'You've got a head cold, or its just a bit of wax,

Lily,' Kate grumbled without opening her eyes and went back to sleep.

Throughout the train journey from Litherland, Lily could hear the single infuriating note in her ear rising and falling in volume. And at one point in the rail journey, Lily thought she distinctly heard a voice calling her name in her affected ear.

'*Lily....Lily...*' the voice was distant, and echoing, and it sounded as if it was a female voice. It sounded quite eerie.

'Of all the days to get this,' Lily thought, and the condition really ruined her working day, because she had to angle her right, good ear, to customers when they made enquiries about the availability of products. Lily worried that her hearing problem would get in the way of any romantic chit chat at her date at the Adelphi, but she needn't have been concerned, because her troublesome ear seemed to clear up when she met up with Rory that night. There was one little cloud on the horizon though – Rory was in the middle of a divorce, he said, and his wife hadn't quite moved out of their flat on Catharine Street. She was deliberately being long-winded about the move out of the flat, according to Rory, just to impede any attempts he made at finding another partner.

Well, after the food and wine and the pouring out of Rory's heart, Lily felt a little light-headed and tipsy, and was filled with that ersatz optimism that often comes from sipping too much alcohol. Rory made it clear he wanted to take Lily home to his flat, and at first this annoyed her – to think that Rory took her as a girl he could bed on the first date –

but then she saw it another way through the haze of intoxication. Rory went out to reception but returned a minute later with a sad smile and a shake of his head. He sat down, grabbed Lily's hand and said: 'I wondered if we could perhaps spend a night here, but the rooms are all booked up, and I've just been told that that's a rarity in this hotel.'

'I feel a bit dizzy anyway with all the wine – ' Lily was saying, when Rory put his square-tipped index finger on the girl's lips to gesture for her to be quiet. He kissed that index finger and then put it back on her lips when she tried to speak again.

He whispered in a low serious voice that conveyed such solemnity: 'I am not living in the shadows of her from now on Lily – you're coming home to my flat – *our* flat.'

And he called for a taxi from the telephone in the hotel lobby, and soon a hackney was taking the couple to Catharine Street. 'Just here's fine,' Rory told the cabby, and the hackney halted near to a red telephone box. When the cabby had been paid, Rory took Lily by the hand and took her into the phone box. 'This is my flat,' he said, with a deadpan expression, 'bit small but the rent's cheap.'

Lily gave a puzzled look, and then Rory grinned and said, 'I'm kidding Lily.'

'Oh, thank God for that,' Lily said, and giggled.

'Look, Lily, I want you to just wait here for a minute – one minute, that's all – and then I'll call you. So when the phone rings, pick it up – it'll be me.'

'I don't get it,' Lily was baffled at this ridiculous arrangement.

'I'll go and see if she's in the flat, and if she isn't, I'll call you, to let you know, and then I'll come down to collect you. If she is in the flat I'll call you and then we'll go elsewhere,' Rory 'explained' and he kissed Lily's forehead and left the telephone box. He hurried up the street, passing the Caledonia pub as he went.

Lily swore to herself under her breath, and then she saw a man appear to the right of the box. He was looking in through the window, and then he began to stare in subdued anger, as if he wanted to make an urgent call. Lily lifted the telephone receiver and stood there with it placed against her ear – her troublesome ear, which had now kicked off again. The man outside said something then stormed off. Lily placed her index and middle finger on the hook so the telephone could receive incoming calls, and she hoped that Rory would ring any moment to say the coast was clear.

'*Lily…*' that uncanny reverberating voice could be heard once again in Lily's blocked ear, as well as a whistling sound. This time the voice was clear because all extraneous noises had been largely cut off in the telephone box. '*Lily…Lily…run….now…get away…please run…now…*' said the voice, and a chill ran down the girl's spine, because she realised whose voice it sounded like. It sounded like the voice of her grandmother Joan, who had died years ago when Lily had just been twelve.

'Gran? Is that you, Gran?' Lily asked, and waited for a reply.

The telephone started to ring, and Lily's fingers released the hook.

'Good news Lily, the coast is C.L.E.A.R!' announced Rory, 'I'm coming down for you.'

Lily panicked, and she dropped the telephone and it swung and hit one of the side windows of the box, and then in blind panic the girl pushed for a few moments on the wrong side of the box, and imagined that the door was stuck, before he realised it was in the other direction. She almost fell out of the telephone box on Catharine Street, and she ran around the corner onto Myrtle Street.

'*Run Lily!*' said the voice in her ear.

'Lily!' Rory's voice sounded in the distance, but Lily couldn't see him when she looked around. She ran towards the Philharmonic Hall, and she could hear heavy running footsteps behind her. She turned and saw it was Rory. His hair was swept back as he ran, and he wore such a hateful expression, and this scared the girl, for she had not seen this facet of his personality before.

'Umph!' Lily ran into someone tall and solid, and fell to the floor.

She found herself at the feet of a policeman. He crouched and helped her up. 'Didn't your mother ever tell you not to look in one direction and run in another?' he said in a monotone voice.

'Officer, help me,' Lily said, out of breath, and she panted the smell of wine into the policeman's face as he helped her up.

'Been drinking, eh?' the constable said, and lifted Lily to her feet in one great vertical yank.

'I need to get away from someone – him!' she said, clinging to the policeman's uniform as Rory stopped dead about twenty feet away.

'He your fellah, is he?' The policeman asked, and then looked at Rory, who was no dabbing his face with a handkerchief as he put on a sincere smile.

'Lily, what's the matter? Why did you run off?' Rory said, and he went up to the frightened girl and put his hand on her forearm, but she pulled away from him and turned to the policeman. 'I don't want to have anything to do with him anymore,' she told the bemused officer of the law.

'It's alright officer, she's been drinking. She always gets like this,' Rory told the copper, and then once again tried to grab Lily's arm. She recoiled away from his heavy-handed grabs.

The policeman shook his head and crossed Myrtle Street to continue on his beat, and Lily shouted after him, 'I don't want to go with him!' And she felt the world tilt. Had Rory put something in her drink or was it just the amount of wine she had imbibed? Lily didn't know.

'Come on, Lily, stop making a scene!' Rory's long muscular arm curled around her shoulder and he rather forcefully pushed her along and now Lily was really afraid. What were his real intentions? Was he going to rape her at the flat?

As Lily was taken back round the corner onto Catharine Street, she heard a female voice shouting her name. She looked left and saw her old schoolfriend Denise and her boyfriend Terry coming over the zebra crossing towards her. The couple were dressed up and obviously going out for the night. Lily saw her chance and she screamed: 'Help! Help!'

Denise was naturally startled by her friend's

screams and she and Terry went to see what the matter was.

'It's okay, she's drunk! Calm down Lily!' Rory told Denise and Terry, but Terry told Rory to let go of the girl, and when he tried to drag her along, Lily let out a scream, and Rory drew back his hand, and was a heartbeat from slapping her, when Terry threw a punch that hit he side of the abductor's head. Rory stumbled against a wall and Lily flew away from him and into the arms of Denise, who was becoming hysterical as her boyfriend got stuck into Rory.

Rory sustained another punch that struck his ear, but he quickly retaliated with a single powerful upper cut to Terry's jaw which left him stretched out cold on his back on the pavement. Denise crouched over her unconscious boyfriend and began to sob as she tried to revive him, and Rory grabbed Lily and dragged her onwards down Catharine Street, and now he began to rant about the trouble women could cause and then he became very incoherent.

The policeman Lily had bumped into earlier was suddenly upon the scene and he tore Rory from the girl and threw him against the wall. The policeman restrained Rory, and then moments later, a police jeep came screeching to a halt on the corner of Caledonia Street and Rory was arrested for causing a disturbance and for the assault on Terry. He was also charged with trying to abduct Lily. It transpired that Rory had a wife at his flat on Catharine Street, but she was not divorced from him at all. Behind his wife's back, Rory had been having affairs with a string of girls, all in their twenties. He had, in his own words, 'been enjoying the best of both worlds.' This was in the days before the Child Support Agency, and Rory discarded many of the girls he saw as 'conquests' when they fell pregnant to him.

Lily was so afraid of meeting Rory again, she left the shop on Bold Street and secured a new job nearer to her home up in Litherland. When she told her mother Kate about the strange warning voice she had heard when her ear was blocked up, Kate revealed a very strange piece of information that had never been told to Lily before. In the 1950s Lily's grandmother had been sexually assaulted at a house on Upper Parliament Street – just around the corner from Catharine Street. This could have all been coincidental, but Lily believes her grandmother somehow tried to warn her about Rory from beyond. Lily has had the odd ear infection since that time in 1977, but has never once heard any strange voices as a result.

THE PACT

I first overheard the following story from two priests when I was an 11-year-old altar boy, and I later researched the incident to unravel a very strange but intriguing account of an attempted exorcism.

There is no sectarianism in Liverpool today (thanks largely to the work of those two late leading lights of Christianity, David Sheppard and Derek Worlock) but it wasn't always so, and I am sure there are still some readers who can remember the dark days when denominations of a religion were used as the basis for discrimination, especially between Catholics and Protestants, and in 1970, this bigotry threatened to hamper an exorcism at a house in Kirkdale. A newly-ordained Catholic priest – Father Kennedy, had been sent for by the mother of a 19-year-old girl said to be possessed by the Devil, and this teen's father – who was of the Protestant faith, sent for the Reverend Blakely to deal with the suspected possession, as he believed that only someone from the Anglican Church could deal with the strange phenomenon he had witnessed.

The girl at the centre of the alleged possession case was Carol, and earlier in the day her mum Theresa had tried to awaken her daughter but found her lying straight as a plank with a bed-sheet wrapped tightly around her. Theresa gently slapped her daughter's face in an effort to awaken her, but to no avail, and then, like many cases of this sort, Carol slowly levitated off the bed and something slapped Theresa hard across her face. An elderly neighbour named Margaret witnessed Theresa being struck with quite some force, and it was this neighbour who immediately decided the Devil was behind the strange goings-on. Margaret suggested a particular priest to Theresa and went with her to their local Catholic church, but the priest they sought was not in the country, and so a priest who had only been ordained a month back agreed to visit Theresa's home. When Father Kennedy arrived at the house, he saw a Church of England priest already in attendance, and this man was the Reverend Blakely.

'We probably won't need the bell, book and candle yet,' Blakely said with a trace of sarcasm in his voice. 'It's quite extraordinary, isn't it?' he asked, squinting at the strange sight before him.

Father Kennedy looked lost when he beheld the surreal spectacle of the levitating girl hanging stock-still in the air, about three feet above her bed, and his fingers fumbled through the pages of his Bible to Psalm 130 – *De Profundis*, which he recited in Latin: 'De profundis clamavi ad te…'

'Leave her alone!' snarled a male voice somewhere close to the priest's ear, making him jump.

The Reverend Blakely was twice the priest's age and calmly asked the entity: 'What do you want with this girl? And who are you?'

No answers came, and Kennedy continued to recite the psalm, all to no effect whatsoever. He and the Reverend went outside onto the landing and looked through the banisters at Carol's distressed family members and neighbours congregating down in the hallway. 'I may have to call in someone more experienced to carry out the Rites of Exorcism,' Kennedy told the Anglican priest, but Blakely was in deep thought and didn't react. After a while he opined: 'I do not think this is any unclean spirit, or any demon.'

Kennedy disagreed and said it had to be the work of Satan, and he opened the bedroom door and looked in at the eerily levitating woman coiled in the blanket. The soles of her bare feet were now curled as if the unconscious woman was suffering from cramp spasms.

'Get out Father Bunloaf!' cried the disembodied male voice again and the door was slammed in the young priest's face.

No progress was made until Blakely quizzed one of Carol's friends – 18 year-old Frances, who told the Reverend a most curious thing. Seven months ago, Carol's boyfriend Christopher had been diagnosed with cancer and had been given a month to live. The cancer had come to light after

Christopher began to feel a numbness in his right leg, and it turned out that the lack of sensation was caused by a tumour on the lad's spine which turned out to be malignant and too advanced to cure. Carol promised Christopher she would kill herself when he died because she couldn't bear being without him. The couple made a pact, and Carol had obtained a bottle of sleeping pills to end her life a day after Christopher died, but couldn't go through with it. Not long afterwards a presence was felt in the girl's bedroom, and Carol also had very vivid dreams in which her boyfriend would urge her to join him in death. Now it all made some sense, and the priests ended up ordering the heartbroken spirit of Christopher to leave the girl he had loved alone. 'You will be reunited with Carol one day, believe me,' Blakely promised, and then came the sounds of a man sobbing. Carol awoke with a scream and fell onto the bed. Christopher never returned. The bond of love between soulmates can even overcome death sometimes, and I can vouch for this, as I have investigated quite a few hauntings where a mother has passed on but is unable to leave her children, as well as cases where children have returned from beyond to feel the embrace of their mothers. I even looked into a case many years ago where a cat that had been savaged by a pit bull terrier returned to play with a Labrador it had been reared with, proving that the bond of love also exists in the world of animals.

EDGE LANE HALL

My *Haunted Liverpool* books are by no means a thorough survey of the supernatural history of my hometown, and I have bulging box-files of places I intend to write about should I find the time to do so. One of these places detailed in the files is Edge Lane Hall, which once stood literally a stone's throw from the Botanic Gardens of Wavertree Park, just across the road from St Sebastian's primary school. The hall had a dark reputation of being one of the most haunted residences in Liverpool, and there were also rumours of a bloodcurdling secret known to one of the families who held residence at the hall for decades. This secret was said to be connected to a very sinister sect of Devil-worshippers who venerated the Fallen One in secret vaults that are known to exist beneath Edge Hill, Wavertree and

Kensington. These vaults, and their eldritch altars are connected by a network of tunnels which were once accessed by a cellar which lies at an incredible depth of over 100 feet below Edge Lane Hall, and they came to light after an investigation by several journalists from the *Liverpool Echo* in April 1913. These tunnels have been surprisingly neglected by our local historians and I can find no references to them in any of the mundane local history books in our libraries and bookshops. Through my own research I have discovered that one tunnel runs beneath Wavertree Park and seems to have an offshoot which goes through sandstone rock towards Edge Hill railway station. Other tunnels are said to go towards the cellars of private residences in Kensington and Edge Hill – possibly the homes of Satanists back in Victorian times. The foundation stone of the hall lies at an incredible and inexplicable depth of two hundred feet. Perhaps there is some connection between the subterranean network of tunnels beneath the hall and the labyrinthine tunnels excavated by the Mole of Edge Hill, Joseph Williamson.

The locals of Kensington, Wavertree and Edge Hill had long regarded the Gothic Edge Lane Hall with its mullioned windows and Norman-inspired architectural features with a suspicious eye, and on some nights, strange chanting voices could be heard coming from the building, and on several occasions screams were heard to emanate from the vaults beneath the hall. There are several reports of police investigating these screams, but all of the investigations came to nothing, perhaps because someone in authority hampered the police inquiries. The screams must have been loud to have been heard at all, as the outer walls of the hall were all 2 feet and 6 inches thick.

During the residency of a prominent banker named Benjamin Arkles, in 1882, a very strange incident took place at Edge Lane Hall. Mary Arkles, the 52-year-old wife of Benjamin, was charged with the task of looking after her two nephews - Peter and Edward, who were aged 9 and 11 respectively – after their mother and father became ill with influenza. One evening, the boys were playing in an upper room of the house, when a deep voice began to talk to them via the chimney. The voice called Peter's name three times, and when Peter asked who was calling, the eerie speaker became silent. Minutes later, the voice said: 'Peter, go outside and look at the moon,' and Peter decided to obey the weird command. He ventured outside with his older brother – and looked up at the unusually large full moon looming over the hall.

'The moon is wobbling,' Peter said, and seemed to go into a trance – and then he began to levitate. He rose slowly from the ground, and as he did, Edward saw a gigantic green vaporous face materialise over Edge Lane Hall, about sixty feet up in the air. This face looked evil, and it grinned as Peter floated up towards it. Edward ran inside the hall to tell his Aunt Mary about the strange goings-on, and she came out with her husband and a religious lodger named Desmond, who began to quote several Psalms from the Bible. The face became contorted at the citing of Holy Scripture and faded away, and

Peter slowly fell back to earth, landing with a gentle bump. The intentions and identity of the face in the sky remain unknown, but Desmond believes the face was that of the Devil, and around this time, the Arkles had heard incantations coming from beneath their cellar. Benjamin Arkles had crucifixes nailed to the walls of the cellar after that spine chilling incident but further spooky episodes took place until the hall was demolished in the spring of 1913. There is a report about Edge Lane Hall in the *Liverpool Echo*, dated Wednesday 16 April, 1913:

LIVERPOOL'S HAUNTED HOUSE
GRIM STORIES OF STRANGE VISITATIONS

The old hall near the Botanic Gardens on the Edge Lane estate is being demolished, and so one of the last remaining historical relics of Liverpool disappears.

At different times of its history the hall has been occupied by several families of local note, but age has woven round it a web of mystery. As in the case with most old buildings it was said to be haunted and certainly the building had all the architectural characteristics which would recommend it as a habitation for a ghost, in the form of secret chambers and subterranean passages.

The hall was for many years occupied by a Mr John de Nash, who acted as caretaker of the mansion for the Corporation of Liverpool, and it was during his tenancy that there was a remarkably strange visitation.

The family were in bed asleep, when suddenly clear, defined and regular came the sounds of chopping wood, and the heavy thud of the axe upon the log; the short, incisive cut of the splinter, or the cracking noise of the splitting stick.

At first the sounds seemed to come from the kitchen, but later they appeared to travel into the hall and up the staircase, ceasing just outside the bedroom door of Mr de Nash. He was a man of courage, and jumping out of bed he lit a candle and, revolver in hand, proceeded to search the house. It was futile, however nothing being found.

On another occasion shortly after midnight there came to the sleepers the sound of a person heavily booted, ascending the stairs. Again the sounds were unmistakable. In great terror the dog ran whining and yelping to the door of the room occupied by Mr de Nash, and lay there trembling in every limb. But not a sign of the heavily-booted person was to be seen. Such noises as these, strange and weird, often broke the silence of the night, and roused the sleeping household.

One rainy morning around 2.40 am in February 2002, a Liverpool cabby was driving his hackney up Edge Lane, carrying two passengers from a nightclub, when he noticed an orange glow to his right. For a moment the taxi driver thought the glow was a fire but soon saw that it wasn't; it was something quite astonishing. A three-storey building he had never seen before stood in the midst of an undulating mist of orange phosphorescent light which resembled a collection of tiny flickering flames. The cabby slowed and then halted his vehicle, and his fares, two girls in their twenties, also saw the strange spectacle. The cabby reached for his phone, intending to take a photograph of the eerie sight, but as he fumbled for the phone, the orange luminance faded and so did thè building with it. This strange apparition had stood on the exact spot where Edge Lane Hall had existed many years before. I later showed a picture of the hall to the cabby and he immediately recognised it as the three-floored residence he had seen surrounded by the glowing mist.

I am still researching the history of the hall and believe it holds many murky secrets which will hopefully come to light soon.

MARY

In 1995, a 24-year-old Kirkby woman named Ellie visited her parent's home in Northwood one Spring afternoon, and her mother told her of a very strange incident.

'Some little girl called here for you today,' said Rita, Ellie's mum, as she made a coffee for her husband.

'What?' Ellie asked with a bemused look. She thought her mother was pulling her leg.

Rita held her hand out, palm facing the floor, to indicate the height of the child she was talking about. 'She was about that tall, big blue eyes, flaxen blonde hair, and she said: "Is Ellie there?" and I said "No" and she stood there, and I asked her what her name was and she just turned and walked off.'

'A kid?' Ellie was baffled at this news.

'She looked as if she was about six or seven years of age. Could she be one of Michelle's kids?' Rita asked her daughter, pouring the milk in the mug of coffee.

'No,' Ellie knew that her friend Michelle over in Southdene only had two girls and they were aged two and three, and they were not blonde-haired. 'You sure she asked for me?'

'She asked for *you*, Ellie,' said Ellie's father from the living room, where he was watching the football with his feet up on the mantelpiece.

'I've never seen blue eyes like that child's eyes,' Rita recalled, stirring the coffee. 'They were huge and bluer than the sky. And she was dressed immaculately, and her clothes looked really expensive.'

Ellie racked her mind trying to think who the child could be who had called for her, and on the following day, after she had returned from college, she went to her flat in the Northwood area of Kirkby and the phone rang. It was her mother Rita. 'She called again about half an hour ago,' she said.

Ellie didn't know who she was referring to for a moment, then realised who her mum was talking about. 'Oh – the kid you mean?'

'Yeah,' Rita told her, 'she asked the same thing, and I asked her what her name was and I asked her what she wanted you for and she just walked away, only this time, your dad followed her, and she disappeared somewhere by Hall Lane. It's a funny one, this, isn't it?'

A few days later, Ellie had to go to the doctor after developing a chesty cough, and as she sat in the doctor's surgery, she heard a voice behind her say, 'Ellie.' Ellie turned and got the shock of her life. There stood a little girl aged about six, with huge baby blue eyes. She wore a long black velvet dress and little well-polished boots. Ellie's stomach turned over. It was Mary, her childhood friend. When Ellie was around 8 years of age she had met Mary near St Chad's and they had become the best of friends. She recalled the day they met, when they linked their little fingers in a bonding ritual. Now, of course, Ellie realised Mary had been a ghost, for she had never gone to her friend's house or met her family and the child always appeared near St Chad's cemetery - the cemetery Ellie had just walked past on her way to the doctor's. The doctor talked to Ellie about antibiotics but she was too mesmerised by the ghost – and it soon became clear the doctor couldn't see Mary, and he thought Ellie was hallucinating the child. 'Why did you stop playing with me?' Mary asked, and Ellie said: 'Because I grew up, and moved house.'

Mary then held out her little hand, pointing her index finger at a startled Ellie. The child stroked her own index finger with her other index finger in a dismissive gesture, and she said: 'Out of friends forever then!' And she started to cry.

'Mary, don't go!' Ellie said, getting up from the chair as the doctor looked on, concerned but intrigued.

Mary turned and ran sobbing through the wall of the surgery, and Ellie looked at the part of the wall the child had vanished into.

'Who's this Mary, eh?' the doctor asked, watching

Ellie dry her tears on the sleeve of her coat.

'It's okay doctor, I'm just feeling run down. I think I need a tonic,' Ellie said, looking at the doctor with red glistening eyes.

Ellie went home and told her mother what had happened, and Rita made the sign of the cross. Her husband, a sceptic in such matters, said the child had not been some ghost, as he had seen her with his own two eyes. Rita and Ellie went to St Chad's that Sunday and said a prayer for the long-dead child.

THE GRINNING MAN SCARE

In December 1963, at a terraced house on Kensington's Saxony Road, a young red-haired housewife named Lindsay was watching her favourite show on television – *Thank Your Lucky Stars* – a highly popular programme that was ITV's answer to *Juke Box Jury*. A panel of celebrities and teenagers gave their views on each pop sensation that mimed its act on the show, and two young regular panellists found fame on this show: a 16-year-old office clerk named Janice Nicholls (who would each week declare in her Black Country accent: "Oi'll give it foive") – and Liverpool's very own Billy Butler. Lindsay had a crush on Billy, even though her mother said that at 30 she was too old for him, and as Lindsay watched *Thank Your Lucky Stars* that Saturday night on 21 December 1963, the housewife thought she saw something out the corner of her eye. She turned towards the window and for a split-second she thought she saw a weird grinning face looking through the window-pane at her. She turned to her father, to see if he had seen the weird face, but he was sitting comfortable in his armchair doing the newspaper crossword as he enjoyed his after-tea smoke. Thinking she had seen a reflection of some sort, Lindsay continued to watch the TV, but once again she saw – via her peripheral vision – that something was at the window, and she turned – only this time the face didn't vanish. It was the face of a bald man, and he was grinning broadly. His face had an unearthly green cast to it, and his eyes looked positively sinister. Lindsay could not see the rest of the body of this uncanny spy; it looked as if just a disembodied head was peering in at her - unless of course, he was wearing a black polo neck sweater. Lindsay screamed and her father looked up, startled – and he too saw the creepy grinning face at the window. The two witnesses then saw the face literally vanish into thin air. This seems to have been an early visitation of the Grinning Man, a weird entity who was seen across Wirral, Liverpool and parts of Lancashire and Cheshire in the 1960s. A very similar entity was also seen in the United States around this time, particularly in the New Jersey area. Days after this, a pale green-faced man with an inane grin on his face was seen looking through the parlour window of a house on Gillibrand Street in Chorley where a wedding anniversary party was going on. Several guests went outside to challenge the Peeping Tom and saw an abnormally tall figure run off at an incredible speed into the night through thick snow. The footprints of this freakish-looking snooper came to an abrupt end in the snow at the end of the street. In January 1967, the Grinning Man was seen again one night around 9pm, peering through the living room window of a house on Norris Green's Stalisfield Avenue. On this occasion, the same pale-green-faced entity with his wide grinning mouth was seen, peering through the net curtains at the family basking in the glow of a roaring fire as they watched television. When the father went to the window and drew back the nets, he saw the nosy parker was at least 6ft 5, and wearing a strange dark one-piece garment similar to a modern-day tracksuit. The lanky figure ran across the garden and effortlessly cleared a 5-foot-tall fence like some latter day Spring-Heeled Jack.

One rainy evening a week later, what seems to have been the same being was seen peering from behind a fence at two teenaged girls on Coronation Road, Crosby as they were returning from a friend's house. The girls ran off in fear and that same night, around midnight, what must have surely been the same 'apparition' was seen skulking about near the cemetery on Portland Street in Southport, and among the witnesses who saw the green-faced figure was a policeman on patrol. He pursued the peculiar-looking stranger but lost him near King Street, where he seemed to vanish into thin air.

The Grinning Man sightings peeked in summer 1968, and one reader – a woman named May, contacted me a few years ago to tell me how, in August 1968, at the age of sixteen, she had been returning from an errand for her mother on Stanley Road, Bootle, when she realised a very tall baldy-headed man was following her. May ran down a dark entry to take a shortcut to her home on Webster Street because she was convinced the lanky stranger was following her. When the girl was half way down this back alley she saw the man she had been fleeing from step out of the mouth of an adjacent entry and look at her with a menacing, grotesque smile. By the feeble light of a nearby lamp the teenager could see that the man's face had a weird green pallor to it, and she screamed, turned on her heels and ran away. She then had to go the long way home and as she passed down Hinton Street, May told a former elderly neighbour named Lizzie about the bizarre and frightening stalker, and Lizzie said other people had seen him earlier in the evening, and she escorted May home. May said that Lizzie told her and her parents that the creepy tall figure with the ghastly smile had been seen near Walton Hospital and nearby Breeze Hill, where two men had given chase, but again the figure had gone to ground rather too fast to have evaded capture by natural means. In 2002 a woman named Betty telephoned me at BBC Radio Merseyside to tell me how she and her daughter had seen the "Grinning Man" I had been discussing on air back in September 1968 on Hawksmoor Road, Fazakerley. Betty and her daughter Carla, who was then just seven, had been returning from a relative's house on Copple House Lane when they saw a long shadow to their left. The shadow, of a head and shoulders, meant that someone was closing in silently behind them, and as it glided silently ahead of the mother and daughter, a faint chuckle was heard. Betty and Carla turned and saw a man in a long black coat which almost touched the pavement. His head was bald and as smooth as an egg, and his face was of a lime-green colour. The eyes were like black horizontal crescents, and the nose was small in contrast to the mouth, which looked unnaturally wide. The grin on the strange man's face was huge and made him look even more baleful and sinister. 'I dragged Carla along as I ran off,' May recalled, 'and we didn't stop running till we reached our house [on Formosa Drive]. My fellah went looking for him but never saw a sign of him anywhere. We later heard the same man had been seen by kids on Aintree Lane.'

The reports of the Grinning Man eventually dried up, and the baffling figure vanished back into obscurity. Just what he was, where he came from, and why he wore that unsettling smile remains a mystery.

AN AIGBURTH ZOMBIE?

The time is near when the dead will be able to speak to us without the involvement of fraudulent, parasitic mediums who prey on those vulnerable people who have lost loved ones. Experiments are taking place east and west on this planet to interface the brains of the dying with sophisticated computers, enabling those 'passing over' to relay a commentary to us in the land of the living, perhaps shedding some light on the fate that awaits every one of us after physical death. The world of forensic science would also benefit from a computer interface to a post-death brain, because we'd be able to replay the sound and vision memory of a murdered person and see and hear the person who had murdered them. Have scientists gone too far in this respect? It's a moot point. Many years ago, footage was smuggled out of the old Soviet Union showing a corpse which raised and lowered its arms when a current was passed through wires running to the motor areas of the dead person's brain. This was a real-life zombie created by scientists who allegedly wanted to develop a zombie army of soulless soldiers who would go into battle minus any conscience or a trace of fear. I have written about rumoured Nazi zombie soldiers the American GIs swore they fought in the twilight days of WWII, and I have also written about reported zombies created by occult means closer to home. Around 1960, a landlord purchased a huge gothic mansion near Fulwood Park, Aigburth, and hired a team of reputable builders to subdivide the palatial property into flats. The builders, however, downed tools when a stomach-churning stench invaded the cellars of the mansion. The smell wasn't from the sewers, and soon there came reports of a terrifying decomposed man who attacked workmen in one cellar and they all fled from this "ghoul", never to return. One builder in his fifties is said to have suffered a stroke during an encounter with the unholy figure which left him without speech for almost a year.

Charles Mordelly, an eccentric 65-year-old ghost-investigator and brother of the renowned self-styled "vampirologist" Victor, was contacted by a friend of the landlord, and the latter paid him to get rid of the thing in the cellar. Charles Mordelly seemed unaffected by the nauseous odour which made the landlord throw up, and in the cellar on the second evening of his investigation, he came face to face with the grotesque source of the mephitis: the tall rotting figure - partly skeletal - of something that had once been a man. The landlord had accompanied Charles to the cellar on this night, but ran off in terror when he saw the ghastly-looking apparition emerging from the tunnel leading into the cellar, and as he fled, the landlord heard a scuffle, loud groans, and gunshots.

Mordelly came up from the cellar minutes later

covered in revolting slime and greyish powder. He claimed he had laid a zombie to rest. Mordelly had researched the previous occupants of the mansion to glean that a sect of extreme occultists had cruelly revived a man from a local graveyard many years ago, possibly in the 1930s, and within this cellar they had carried out one of the most dangerous resurrection rites known in the world of the occult to reanimate the man, but instead some evil spirit, hungry to live again, had possessed the revivified corpse.

The landlord saw the powdery outline of the so-called zombie on the cellar floor and said he found the tale of 'resurrection' hard to believe, but Mordelly, angered at being doubted, said: 'What about Lazarus of Bethany? Do you doubt that he was raised from the dead by Jesus?'

The landlord never answered, but paid Mordelly for his work, and on the following day the landlord had the entrance to a mysterious tunnel (which ran under Jericho Lane) sealed up. The part of Fulwood Park where the occultists had their base in the 1930s saw increased supernatural activity during their tenancy. Fulwood House, which was then Fulwood Lodge, was plagued with poltergeist activity, and the ghosts of several Victorian children and a woman in black also came out of the paranormal woodwork for a while.

HAUNTING MELODIES

On the Monday morning of November 29, 1920, a young Liverpool man named Jim Sterry left his lodging house in North Woolwich, London and boarded a double-decker bus to take him to work. He went upstairs to the top, open deck of the bus to have a smoke, and sitting a few seats in front of Jim was a friend. This young man said hello to Jim and then he began to sing a popular tune called *O Death Where is They Sting?* This song was written by Clarence A. Stout – who took the title of his composition from a quote in the Bible's Corinthians, and the number had been made a hit on both sides of the Atlantic by the talented black comedian and crooner Bert Williams. The young man was just singing the part of this song that runs: 'Why hell is full of vampire women, whisky, gin, and dice, make Satan get behind thee, now prepare for paradise – ' when something flew across the Thames and smashed into the singer's head, killing him instantly. Screams rented the air and women fainted at the gruesome sight. It transpired that, moments earlier, parts of the steam turbine at Woolwich Power Station had disintegrated when a speed-governing device failed. In the resulting explosion, a section of the turbine blades had been thrown across the Thames to kill the young man seated on the open top deck of the bus. Relatives of the victim of this freak tragedy said the young man had been singing *O Death Where is Thy Sting?* for days and said he couldn't get the song out of his head, and the superstitious naturally wondered: was that song some dark portent of the lightning decapitation of the victim? Songs that you can't get out of your head rattle around the mind because they are catchy – at least that's what any psychologist would reason, but despite the theories of Freud, Jung, Lorenz and Skinner, the unconscious mind is as unchartered as it was in the days of Homer, and its secret workings continue to mystify. I have discovered a whole branch of the paranormal where songs and poems that people have not heard for years suddenly begin to haunt their waking minds, and these songs and verses don't always seem significant at first – until some skirmish with death or some nerve-jangling news arrives – and the verses become chillingly relevant. Take, for example, Jackie Johnson, who woke up one sunny morning in June 1960 with the 1941 Ink Spots song *I Don't Want to Set the World on Fire* playing in her mind's ear. That song haunted her into the afternoon, even as she shopped in the popular Church Street store Hendersons, which was engulfed by a blaze which killed eleven people that day. Jackie was one of the lucky ones who ran out the building when she first saw the smoke billowing through the store. Only afterwards did Jackie's mother realise the significance of the song that had become 'stuck' in her daughter's head.

In March 1980, Jean Harris, a school headmistress in the United States, murdered her lover Herman Tarnower, and a psychiatric evaluation of Harris revealed how the song *Put the Blame On Mame* played non-stop in her mind, and continued to do so till she died 32 years later. In February 2005 a Tuebrook woman named Liza woke up one morning and was plagued by Men At Work's 1983 hit *Down Under*, and that same day out of the blue, her husband landed a job in Sydney, and he and his family later moved to Australia.

Maybe we should pay more heed to these "warning songs"...

SOME VIOLENT LIVERPOOL GHOSTS

I spend hours researching strange phenomena in libraries and various newspaper archives, and recently, whilst perusing an old yellowed copy of *The Nottingham Evening Post*, dated Friday, April 8, 1932, I came upon the following article on page nine:

VIOLENT "GHOST"

Woman Lifted Over Banisters and Dropped!
Weird Happenings in Georgian House

An astonishing series of ghostly incidents are alleged to have occurred in a Liverpool house.

A man states that he was flung downstairs, and a woman asserts that she was lifted bodily over the banisters and dropped to the floor. The woman was taken to hospital suffering from severe bodily injuries and nervous trouble.

The house is an old Georgian structure which was recently occupied by several families.

On the night of occupation a house-warming party heard strange noises. The party disbanded and a search was made but nothing was found.

During the next three nights unearthly sounds were heard, and the men decided to inform the police. They were leaving the top rooms when there was a crash, and a man was found at the bottom of the stairs. He asserted that he did not slip.

The climax came on the fourth night. Some families were preparing to take out the furniture, and men went upstairs, followed by the eldest of the women. Suddenly a woman screamed when at the top of the stairs, and she was seen to go over the banisters and fall to the hall floor.

All concerned assert that she appeared to be lifted bodily over the banisters, surrounded by a strange illumination. The woman, who is conscious, yesterday stated that that she felt herself lifted by invisible hands.

Although the house in question is not identified in the newspaper, it matches almost identical accounts I have in my files to the Sackville Street haunting, in which a particularly violent ghost began to attack people who had moved into a house in Everton's Sackville Street that had long lain empty. In that case, which also took place in 1932, a woman was lifted over the banister and dropped, almost breaking her neck. A number of curious people who ventured into the house during the ghost scare were seen to sail down flights of stairs in mid-air by an invisible force that threw them against walls in the hallway. These types of ghost – which inflict physical harm – are thankfully in the minority, but they *are* around in Liverpool and beyond, and what follows are just a few examples of aggressive apparitions.

In the early 1960s an elderly man came into Bootle's police station on Oriel Road in a confused state. He said a group of young noisy people had moved into his house. The old man – who identified himself as Mr John Fay, a retired commercial traveller, said he had lived at his address on Trinity Road for over 20 years. 'Are the young people squatting in your home sir?' asked the sergeant on desk duty at the station, and he noticed how nervous Mr Fay was.

'They just came into my home and now they won't go, and they are so noisy and – ' Mr Fay was saying, when in walked a young constable. This baby-faced policeman was told to go to the address given by Mr Fay to see what was going on. In the meantime, the sergeant at the desk brought the old man a mug of cocoa to try and calm his nerves. Almost a quarter of an hour passed, and the young policeman returned to the station on Oriel Road - and he found his colleague alone and white-faced at the desk. 'Where's Mr Fay gone?' the youthful constable inquired, and the older sergeant behind the desk said: 'He disappeared.'

'Where to, sir?'

'Into thin air – he was a ghost,' replied the sergeant, wide-eyed, and he looked at the untouched mug of cocoa on the counter, then told the constable how the man had started ranting and raving about the young people who had moved into his home, and as he seethed, the old man became see-through a few times. When the sergeant had said, 'Jesus Christ you're a spirit,' the old man had made a grunting sound and then he had vanished before his eyes.

This now made sense to the young constable, because he had gone to the address given by Mr Fay on Trinity Road and found the young "squatters" there to be a rather peaceful lot. They had admitted the constable in and showed him rent books to prove that they were the rightful and legal tenants. It later came to light that a Mr Fay had died at the address on Trinity Road many years before, and that his ghost had been seen on the premises of his former home on many occasions. People didn't last long at the address because Fay's ghost was very violent and he would throw objects at people living in 'his' home and on one occasion he had tried to strangle a woman in her bed. Two priests were brought in to exorcise the ghost in the end, and even the holy men had a rough time when something threw pepper in the eyes of one priest and whipped the back of another priest with a poker. The Rites of Exorcism were carried out successfully in the end and the ghost of John Fay – as far as I am aware – never returned to his old home on Bootle's Trinity Road.

One of the most sinister as well as violent cases of

supernatural assaults I researched concerned a beautiful-looking house in Falkner Square. In the early 1970s a family of four – a doctor, George, his wife, Anne, and their children Paul, aged three and Matthew aged eight, moved into the house and soon settled into their new residence. A nanny named Lucy was later hired to look after the children when Anne took up a teaching job in a well-known Liverpool girls' school, and it was shortly after Lucy's arrival when the first incidences of ghostly goings-on took place. George and his wife returned home around 5.45pm and were told by the nanny that someone had been moving the furniture, ornaments and books around in the lounge. George suspected his son Matthew at first, but a few days later when Matthew was still at school, Lucy found that every volume of the doctor's *Encyclopaedia Britannica* had been rearranged so that the volumes began with Z and ended in A. Three Royal Doulton figures had been turned on their shelf to face the wall, and the doctor's collection of African tribal masks from the Ivory Coast hung from the wall at odd angles. On the following day, which was a Saturday, Lucy and the doctor's wife Anne took the boys out to the fairground at New Brighton, and on several occasions during this period, the doctor heard noises in his study. The first noise was a thumping sound, and the doctor went into his study but saw nothing to account for the thud. Minutes after this, the doctor switched on the television to watch the BBC sports programme *Grandstand*, then went into the kitchen to make himself a coffee and a sandwich. When he returned to the lounge he noticed the door to his study was wide open, even though the doctor clearly remembered closing it. He went inside and saw that all six drawers of his Edwardian mahogany desk were open, and this naturally spooked George. He was a doctor, a man of logic and science and rational thought who had no belief in the supernatural, but what he was experiencing was inexplicable. He closed the drawers, and closed the door of the study, then went and sat on the sofa in the lounge and kept looking at the study door now and then as he tried to watch *Grandstand*. He never told his wife Anne or the nanny Lucy about the weird incidents in case it alarmed them, but later that night, at around 11pm, something terrifying took place at the house. Screams from the boys' bedroom pierced the air, sending George, Anne and Lucy upstairs to the second floor. As George barged into the bedroom of his children, he saw several toys – Corgi and Dinky cars and an Action Man doll - tracing an unnatural parabola as they sailed through the air across the room. The toys seemed to land in slow motion on the carpeted floor with gentle thuds. Such inertial behaviour is a signature of the poltergeist. Stones and various objects thrown by these 'spirits' have been known to fall unnaturally slow and to prescribe elongated arcs and bizarre trajectories.

Matthew was hysterical, and he ran to his mum and dad talking excitedly and incoherently about 'two boys' who had come into the room out of a cupboard to fight him. The lad's younger 3-year-old brother Paul was sitting up in his little bed and rubbing his eyes as if he had just woken up. The doctor assured his son he had only had a bad dream, and that there were no strange boys in his room. Lucy opened the cupboard the boys were supposed to have come from and Matthew clung to his mother with wide-eyes as he gazed at the cupboard in terror, but the nanny smiled uneasily and showed the frightened child that there was nothing untoward in the cupboard, just clothes hanging on a rail.

There were no further incidents that night, but on the following day during the afternoon, Lucy was about to leave the house with little Paul for a Sunday stroll around the park in the centre of Falkner Square, when the boy suddenly halted in the hall and pointed up a flight of stairs with a beaming smile. 'Look, Lucy! There are those naughty boys!' he shouted, and Lucy looked up the stairs and saw no one standing up on the landing, but the nanny had the creepy feeling she was being watched, and was only too glad when she stepped outside the house into the sunshine.

As the nanny took Paul for a walk in the park, she asked him about the "naughty boys" and he told her they were the boys who had broken Matthew's toys and hit him. Lucy could get no more information about the boys from Paul, but she told the child's mother what he had said when she returned to the house.

In the following week, on a Wednesday night at around 11.40pm, Matthew awoke in his darkened bedroom, and he could clearly hear voices. They were wells-spoken voices, but childish voices, perhaps belonging to someone his own age group or perhaps a little older. Matthew reached out and turned on his bedside lamp, and there, at the foot of his bed, he saw the two boys who had thrown toys at him and struck him on the Saturday night. They were dressed in identical blazers with black and yellow "deckchair" stripes and they both wore the same schoolboy-style caps, shorts, and green woollen socks. The strange boys looked like twins, and both had round faces with rosy cheeks and were quite fat. As they turned to face Matthew, the boy saw that one of the schoolboys held a cricket bat and the other held what looked like a hockey stick. The creepy duo grinned simultaneously, and then one of them shouted 'He's awake!' and he began to strike the end of the bed with the cricket bat, injuring Matthew's ankles through the duvet. Matthew let out a scream as the second boy began to strike his head with the hockey stick, and the doctor's son saw flashes of light each time the stick belted his skull. Matthew rolled out the bed and held up the duvet in a desperate attempt to cushion the blows, but then he felt himself being kicked in the legs, and groin. He then heard Paul screaming hysterically, and this enraged Matthew and he tried to get up, but he heard one of the unearthly intruders swear at him and he received a punch in his ear. The boys roared with laughter and ran towards the cupboard, and seconds later, Matthew heard running sounds outside the door. It was his father, mother and nanny coming up the stairs. The door burst open and the doctor rushed to his son's aid as Anne let out a scream. On this occasion, the cupboard in the corner, which, according to Matthew, the two boys came from, looked as if it had been pulled a few inches from the wall, and one of its doors was open. Lucy thought she saw the grinning face of a boy looking out from behind the partially opened door and yelped. When the doctor looked in the cupboard seconds later there was nothing there.

The doctor heard Matthew's spine-chilling account of the wicked boys in the striped blazers, and then he asked Paul what he had seen, and the boy was too upset to talk until almost an hour later, when he said the boys had slapped his face in the dark. He had also seen them at the window, presumably as silhouettes.

Suspecting that Matthew had sustained a fractured skull, his father called an ambulance and had him taken to hospital where the boy was X-rayed, and luckily the injuries to his head were not serious, but Matthew was not allowed to sleep until morning because he was suffering from a mild form of concussion.

Enough was enough. The boys were put in a room on the ground floor from then on, and there were no more visits from the ghostly boys, but every now and then, something would rearrange the furniture, shuffle the books on the shelves, and on a few occasions there were loud knocks on the front door in the dead of night. In the end, the doctor decided to move to a house on Menlove Avenue, and I hear that the house in Falkner Square is still haunted, although I have not heard of anyone in the house having encounters with the schoolboys. Just who they are is still unknown. Falkner Square dates back to the 1830s and many illustrious and well-to-do families lived there over the years; who knows what tragedies and strange tales have taken place within the walls of those grand townhouses? I know of many ghosts within Falkner Square, but none of them are as violent as "Tweedledee and Tweedledum".

THE DABBLERS

One calm frosty spring morning in 1968, two workers on a building site in Speke were carrying a stacked shutter board along the guard board forty-feet up among the scaffolding erected around the rising structure of a semi. Murphy was at one end of the long shutter board and Peters was at the other, and he was tiring of Murphy's continual gabbing. 'I just know that I'll win the Pools one day soon, and when I do I'm moving to a place called Hart in the north-east of Hampshire –' Murphy was saying when he and Peters were suddenly lifted by a tremendous howling, cyclonic gust of wind which caught the shutter board. The two men became airborne and went sailing over the platform railing in an unnatural arced trajectory which brought them down gently on the corrugated roof of the site office.

The brickies, plasterers, plumbers, electricians navvies and even old Mr Hammond, the Clerk of Works, laughed out loud at the vertical take-off and landing. Murphy swore it was no freak gust of wind that had lifted him and Peters off the scaffold on such
a calm day.

'Here we go,' Mike Heath, fastest bricky in Lancashire remarked, as Murphy claimed supernatural forces had levitated him. Murphy always seemed to bring up the subject of ghosts and spirits whenever anything remotely odd arose. The men had come into work a few mornings ago and found eight planks laid out as a swastika – obviously the work of youths who had climbed over the wire fence surrounding the site. But Murphy believed the Nazi symbol was the work of some local cult.

At lunch, a strange rumour circulated in the canteen; that another firm of builders had refused to excavate this site because it had a bad reputation for being haunted, and Murphy, upon hearing this uncanny claim, told his sceptical friends: 'I knew it – I sensed it as soon as I set foot on this site – it's unholy – unhallowed ground they call it! I told you that was no wind that lifted me and Peters up, but you all thought it was old superstitious Murphy talking shite'.

Mike Heath asked Mr Hammond about the validity of the 'haunted site' story and was surprised at the reply he received from the Clerk of Works: 'Well, yes, Mike, it is true that the workers thought the site was haunted, but then I heard many of them were drunks and a bunch of superstitious idiots. It's 1968, not 1368, but yes, some lead-swinger said the site was cursed and that was it – off they went.'

Mike shook his head but had a pensive look as he sipped his coffee.

'You don't believe in all that mumbo jumbo do you?' Mr Hammond asked with a lopsided grin.

Mike shrugged and admitted he had never seen a ghost but remained open-minded about life after death.

After the freak wind incident, more strange incidents took place on the site. A bricklayer's labourer went up a ladder with a full hod and was grateful when some colleague unburdened him of his load at the top of the ladder, but when he looked up, the hod was empty and no one was about. The bricks were arranged in a cube on the ground. The hod-carrier almost fell down the ladder in his quick descent.

Not long after that, an old spindle-back chair in the site office became very affectionate towards Mr Hammond and was seen to slide after him, giving the clerk a funny turn. Mick Heath saw the 'walking chair' and was more intrigued than afraid, but Mr Hammond had the chair removed from the office. On the following morning it was found on the office desk, even though the site office hut had been locked when that chair had been left over by the feeder skip, about seventy yards away.

A creepy atmosphere descended on the site, especially now that there had been a change in the fine spring weather. Heavy masses of grey cumulus cloud gathered and hung low over Speke, and in the gathering gloom, many of the workmen began to notice a sweet sickly aroma of the type that lingers in graveyards, believed to be formed by the mingling of wilting grave flowers and bodily decomposition odours filtering up through the clay.

A glazier swore that someone invisible to his eyes had touched him on the left shoulder twice as he installed panes in a window, and a tough navvy who had worked as a formidable bouncer said he'd had enough and handed in his cards after bumping into something that wasn't there. Murphy lapped all this up and was about to amplify the suspense by recalling some alleged ghostly incident, when Mr Hammond berated him and warned him he'd be sacked on the spot unless he shut up and continued with his work. Murphy stormed off in a huff and grabbed a wheelbarrow.

About half an hour after this, an electrician named Bernie noticed the eerie sounds of what sounded like a distant choir, but this choral group were singing some sort of hymn no one had ever heard before. The plumbers heard it, and thought it was coming from below ground, and then Mike Heath heard it and said it was probably a school choir somewhere in the distance. 'Sound can travel on the wind on days like this,' Heath said, but no one was having it. There came a rumble of thunder and a downpour of pelting rain. Canvas covers were brought out, but the rain stopped, and the promise of an early dart evaporated.

The ghostly singers were heard again, and Mr Hammond came out of his office hut and asked if someone had a transistor radio on, because he could hear the choir as well. When he saw that no one had a radio on, he turned to Mike and asked to see him in his office. Mike went into the hut and Hammond said he had heard footsteps walking past his desk about half an hour ago. 'Heavy footsteps, they were, and they went from one corner of this room to the other, and I also heard a swishing sound as it went past the desk,' Hammond told Heath.

'Does anyone know what stood on this spot years ago?' Heath asked.

'There was nothing here, just open land,' Hammond told him, 'not even farm land. I know what you're thinking, but no, there was no old Tudor house here or anything.'

Mike then made a very controversial suggestion. 'Maybe we should try and contact the thing that's causing all the disruptions.'

'How do you mean?' Hammond took off his glasses and cleaned the lenses with a tissue.

'A ouija board,' Heath replied meekly, and looked down at his rough hands, expecting the Clerk of Works to ridicule the suggestion.

'They're supposed to be very dangerous aren't they?' Hammond said, putting his glasses back on. His eyes looked sharp and stern. 'Do they work?'

Heath shrugged and said he had heard stories about them. 'I've heard that they're very dangerous but well, I don't know.'

'It might be worth a try,' Hammond seemed to have become a convert to spiritualism since he had experienced the dancing chair and heard the phantom walker.

'We should get a priest in – get him to bless the site,' Heath suggested.

Hammond sat and grimaced at the suggestion. 'I don't think a priest would do that in this day and age, and if we start bringing in the Church, the men might think there really is something evil knocking about.'

About half an hour before knocking-off time, eleven men gathered around a table in the canteen and seven of them took part in the Ouija session, all placing rough square-tipped fingers on the upturned glass in the centre of a ring of letters cut from various newspaper headlines. Heath told the participants that this session was just an experiment, and tried to be a bit light-hearted about it. The men were understandably nervous, and Heath kicked off the proceedings: 'Okay, let's see if any spirits are about,' he said, and after a pause, he asked: 'Where is Billy Lawson?'

Some of those sitting around smiled and asked who Lawson was, and Heath said it was the name of his brother-in-law who had mysteriously deserted his wife 3 years back. He had not been seen since, and no one could trace him.

The glass slid about and spelt out "BROWN BREAD" – a rhyming slang word Lawson habitually used to mean "dead".

This response from the Ouija gave Heath quite a start, and he accused people of pushing the glass but all the sitters said they weren't messing about.

'Okay, let's try another one,' Mike Heath said as he looked up into the mid-air above the table. 'Are there spirits on this building site?'

The glass sped so fast back and forth across the table, it flashed and traced a triangle as it spelt out the letters: 'Y-E-S'.

One of the men swore under his breath, and Heath noticed that the plumber was clutching the beads of a Holy Rosary.

'How many spirits are here?' Heath asked, and this time the Ouija didn't respond immediately. There was a pause of about a minute, and then again the glass zigzagged about, and spelt out the words: 'A-L-O-T'.

'A lot eh? How many is that?' Heath queried, and he and many present felt the table vibrate at a very low frequency when this question was posed.

Heath was just about to ask another question when the glass began to dart to and fro inside the circle of paper letters, and a man named Marty, who was writing the results of the Ouija pointer down in a notebook said: 'I didn't get that, it's moving too fast. It looked like it was spelling out G-O-A-W-A-Y'.

The glass moved again and spelt out several swear words, and then, whatever was moving the glass spelt out fourteen letters: JWJPQRMHAMSSDH – and when everyone took their fingers off the glass it continued to move along at a snail's pace, then slid off the table and smashed on the floor.

Later that day, Murphy realised the 14 letters were the initials of the seven men who had laid their fingers on the Ouija glass, and within days, the first on the list John Williams, died in a car crash. Then Jim Peters dropped dead of heart failure, and Quentin Rogers contracted pneumonia and was said to be hovering at the gates of death in a hospital ward. Mike Heath was next on the list, and he tried everything to repel the influence of the thing he perceived as some malevolent spirit. Mike seemed to become unhinged, and got the carpenters to erect a huge cross made from planks, even though Hammond tried to talk them out of it. It seemed as if a mania had gripped the workforce of the site. The cross was erected and Murphy painted the words: 'Jesus is Lord' on a large piece of plasterboard and hung it from the scaffolding. Mike Heath also bought Bibles from a religious bookshop and placed them at the four corners of the site and took to carrying holy water from a church in a bottle. Tense days went by, and nothing harmful happened to Heath, and thankfully nothing bad happened to the other four men on that accursed list. Years after this incident, the claims of the Ouija spirit regarding Heath's brother-in-law were proven to be true when it was found that Billy Lawson had committed suicide shortly after he left his wife in Colchester. Lawson overdosed on sleeping pills and was later found in a park.

The house built by the workmen on that haunted site still stands in Speke, and it has been noted that around every seven years, there is an outbreak of poltergeist activity on the premises which always starts after a sweet sickly odour invades the rooms.

LONG ARMS

When I was researching my book *Beasts, Banshees & Bogeymen* a few years back, I was looking desperately for information on the bogeyman featured in the following story, but all of the accounts I collected from readers came in too late to be included in the book. I have no idea what is behind the stories of Long Arms, but perhaps when I get more accounts in I might be able to determine whether he was merely the results of pranksters or a genuine paranormal entity.

In the summer of 1974, singer-songwriter Ray Stevens had a hit with *The Streak* - a novelty song about an opportunistic streaker who wears nothing but his tennis shoes. The song was released at the peak of a streaking mania which had started in the universities of the USA a few years before as a bit of tomfoolery, although there are reports of streakers in the press in London and Liverpool as early as 1799. All of these streaks were carried out by young people for dares and wagers, but back to the halcyon summer of 1974 in Liverpool's Everton district, for in that year, a woman in her seventies streaked; we shall call her Mary. What was Mary's motive for divesting of her clothes that July? It wasn't the tepid heat of that mediocre summer, so perhaps the motivation was an act of rebellion against ageing, a last stand against the iron law of senescence – or perhaps it was just for fun – we'll never know now. Anyway, Mary streaked from the corner of Mere Lane and Heyworth Street to the corner of Breck Road, and obviously caused quite a stir. Some saw the funny side of a septuagenarian streaker running about in her birthday suit, but some of the more puritanical flint-faced people of Everton thought it was downright disgusting.

'The men in the white coats will be coming for her,' June, Mary's neighbour predicted, and June's son, 13-year-old Tony said he'd heard that Mary was planning to streak again through Paddy's Market. June made the sign of the cross, and went and told half the street what Tony had heard, and the resulting wave of gossip rippled through the purlieus of Everton and beyond. Adults and children began to frequent Mary's neighbourhood to catch the old streaker in the act, and around this time, another, weirder rumour gained currency: a sinister man in a black mackintosh and black trilby had been seen stalking children in the alleyways of Everton and parts of Anfield, and this man had all the makings of a modern bogeyman, because, according to the many reports, he had arms that could stretch abnormally and extend several feet to grab the kids he hunted, and whenever adults gave chase, the telescopically-limbed stranger would go to ground too fast to be of this world. June warned her son about this "Long Arms" as he was nicknamed, and Tony mocked his mother's credulity, and Tony's dad Arthur also giggled at his wife's gullibility, quipping, 'Everton could do with him in goal – long arms!'

'Listen Doubting Thomas,' June addressed her hubby, 'Mrs McCarthy saw him on Conway Street trying to grab her lad; why would she lie?' And Arthur hid behind the broadsheet *Liverpool Echo* and whispered profanities as he read the cinema guide.

That very night, under a full moon that gilded the streets of Everton with its quicksilver radiance, Tony was having 'a game of war' with a stick for a machine gun as he ran down an entry off Great Homer Street. Two mates hurled imaginary grenades at Tony and did all the usual accompanying vocal sound effects of machine guns, flame-throwers, bazookas and whistling shells. Tony, being indestructible, ran on unharmed and vanished round a corner, and never emerged again until his worried friends went in search of him. Perhaps it was all a ruse for an ambush, the kids wondered, but then they found him, leaning against a backyard wall, holding his bruised throat with tears in his eyes.

Tony said he had run into "Long Arms" and had almost been strangled by him. He had been running past the backyard doorway of a "bombdy" – a derelict house when he suddenly noticed a man in a long black coat and a tribly standing in the doorway of the yard, and as Tony realised who he was, the man's arm reached out in a way no normal human arm could, because it extended at least six feet or more, even though the man was of average height. Then in an instant, Tony felt a strong hand close around his throat, and it squeezed so much he couldn't cry out. He almost lost consciousness as the gloved hand – which only had four digits – squeezed his windpipe like a vice. Two older lads passing through the entry saw Tony being throttled and came to help him, and the man ran into the backyard of the empty house and vanished.

'Long Arms!' one of Tony's mates gasped, realising who the attacker had been.

And then came the distant sounds of running feet. The trio turned to see where the running sound was coming from, and they soon noticed that a man in a long black mack and a dark trilby was racing towards them from the top of the entry, about a hundred yards away – and his black gloved hands were almost touching the floor as he closed in on them. The kids ran off in terror, and all three fought to be at the front and for a moment they all became jammed in the entry as the creepy assailant got closer.

Tony told his parents what had happened, and although his mother believed him and wanted to take him to the police station to report the sinister fiend, her husband Arthur forbade her to take Tony to the police, warning her that she'd make herself and him a laughing stock. Arthur accused his son of making up the story of the attack, and Tony went and got the family Holy Bible, placed his hand on it rather melodramatically, and swore on it. 'I swear I was attacked tonight by some thing with dead long arms! There, Doubting Thomas!' he cried at his sceptical father.

'May God strike you down if you're lying!' Arthur yelled back at him, and paused and looked at the ceiling as if he expected a lightning bolt to come through it on its way to strike Tony.

Some said Long Arms was just a prankster with gloves on the end of poles, but Tony and others who encountered the weird entity knew otherwise. The last report of this bogeyman – or whatever he was - was around 1982 on Latham Street, where Long Arms is said to have chased a gang of children in broad daylight. Several motorists are said to have seen the uncanny long-armed figure running after the hysterical children. We hopefully will find out more one day about this Liverpool bogeyman of the 1970s and early 1980s.

A NORRIS GREEN HAUNTING

Netherwood Road in Norris Green is a fairly typical road of terraced and semi-detached homes, running for about 270 yards between Townsend Avenue and the square of Abbotsford Road. In the early 1990s there was a strange haunting at one of the houses on Netherwood Road, and the main witness to the terrifying goings-on had ironically been what clichéd writers on the paranormal would call a 'hardened sceptic'. Harry had been divorced from his wife in the 1980s, and now, in his mid-fifties he decided to move to a terraced home on Netherwood Road which was remarkably cheap, and the plan was to build a life again within this house with a woman nearer his own age, unlike his ex, who had been almost twenty years his junior. Hopefully, Harry would meet someone and settle down in Norris Green, but not long after he had moved into the house, he realised why it had been so cheap. He got talking to the neighbours, and learned that their 13-year-old daughter was having a terrible time sleeping because something was keeping her awake at nights, and that something was thought to be a ghost in Harry's loft. This naturally shocked Harry. He was now working nights at a filling station, and was getting home around 7am most mornings, and so he was obviously missing all of the supernatural action, which, according to the neighbours, commenced around 11pm and always seemed to end around five in the morning.

Harry's nephew, a clever 16-year-old named Nathan, said he could make a tape recorder that switched itself on at a preset time – and this would mean the tape could record the ghostly activity while Harry was at work. Harry wasn't too keen on this experiment, because he had never in all of his fifty-odd years ever experienced anything remotely supernatural and he thought ghosts were all in the mind. Working long nights at the filling station he had seen nothing in the lonely watches of the night, and when the odd ghost story was told by some DJ on Radio City, he would change stations and listen to Radio Two. Nathan turned up with the cassette recorder and a timer that plugged into the mains outlet. His father used the timer to switch on lamps when the family were out, to supposedly deter burglars. Anyway, Nathan set the timer and tape recorder in a spare bedroom and taped a microphone with an extended lead (created by the cellotaping of various wires) to a lamp shade so that the mike would be near to the ceiling. Now any spooky noises in the loft would be clearly captured when the ghost walked.

Harry went to work at 10pm and spent most of

the time at the filling station serving the occasional night driver and usual drunks craving sandwiches, cigarettes and mineral water. The regulars also made their usual nocturnal visits in the wee small hours; the talkative opinionated cabbies, an agoraphobic who would only come out at 3am to buy a £5 electric token and so on. It was a pretty uneventful stretch, and on this occasion Harry read an old Sven Hassel paperback to make the long hours bearable. He must have thought of the tape recorder in the spare bedroom about once.

At 6.30am he was driving home to Netherwood Road, and as he approached the front door, he heard a strange rhythmic sound: Gok! Gok! It sounded as if someone was chopping wood in his back garden. Was some low life breaking into his home? Harry fumbled with the keys, went into the house, keyed in the predictable four-digit code – 1066 – to disable the alarm – and went into his kitchen, where he could now clearly hear the chopping sound. He gingerly opened the door to the back garden and the security light flooded everywhere with its halogen luminence.

There was a long axe – just like a fireman's axe – embedded in the old table that had been there since when he first bought the house, and on the floor, next to the table, were the chopped-up remains of two benches that had been part of that old outdoor table. Where did that axe come from? Harry had never seen it before, and no one could have left the garden in between the sound of the last fall of that axe blade and the time the security light had come on.

Harry was that scared, he went back into the house and waited until it was light before he would venture out into the back garden again. He put the long-handled axe in the back-garden shed and locked it up. He then went to bed, and around 3pm he got up, and after some tea and toast, he went up to the spare bedroom and brought the tape recorder down to the living room. The cassette length was 45 minutes, and he could hear nothing but the usual hiss of white noise, plumbing sounds, as well as the odd drone of an aircraft passing overhead or the sound of a car travelling down Netherwood Road – and then, around fifteen minutes into the tape, Harry could hear the sounds of someone walking heavy on what seemed to be wooden boards. This unknown walker seemed to be pacing up and down somewhere. Harry switched it off because he found the sounds unnerving, even though he didn't believe in ghosts. Nathan turned up at teatime and asked if the tape had recorded anything and Harry told him it had, and the boy naturally wanted to listen to the recording of the footsteps but Harry told the boy to take the tape and the cassette recorder home, along with the timer. He didn't want to hear the unexplained noises again because the phenomenon ran against everything he believed in.

The shifts changed at the filling station, and on Saturday, Harry was put on mornings. He would now have to get to the station at 6.30am and work till 2.30pm in the afternoon for a week. And so, Harry went to bed at normal hours. He deliberately turned the volume on the TV up around 11pm, mindful of the neighbours stories about the noisy ghost that started to walk in his loft at that time. At half-past midnight, Harry decided to go to bed, and climbed the stairs to his bedroom. As he walked up the stairs he heard the faint sounds of chopping wood again, and halted. It was definitely that sound he had heard the night he had seen the long-handled axe embedded in the table in the back garden, but he was too afraid to investigate, and he hurried up the stairs and went to bed. He left the light on and turned on the little alarm-clock radio on his bedside cabinet. He also began to browse a Sunday magazine supplement to take his mind off the distant thudding sounds of the ghostly wood-chopper. The light started to flicker, and then went out, and the alarm-clock radio, being mains operated, also died. Harry swore, more with nerves than frustration, and he reached for his lighter and clicked it. He then went down the stairs shielding the lighter's fragile flame with his cupped hand, and all the while he could hear two things; the rhythmic sound of the axe chopping wood, and the screams of the neighbours' daughter next door. He located a torch in the kitchen and switched it on. The bulb lit but seemed weak. By its feeble light Harry located the fuse box – and saw that every fuse was okay – so why had the lights gone out? He found a pack of unopened batteries and put them in the torch. Now the beam was much brighter. Harry examined every fuse once again in case he had overlooked one blown one, but now he was absolutely sure that the fuses were intact. He went back up to the bedroom with the torch, and by now the girl next door had calmed down. Harry undressed to just his Y-fronts, and got into bed. He opened the curtains as wide as possible, to allow some of the sickly amber light from the sodium lamp post into the room. He then lay in bed with the duvet almost covering his head, and yet he could still faintly hear the wood-chopping sound. So many thoughts of the ghost came crowding into his mind as he lay there. Who was haunting the house? What was the significance of the axe? Would it come and visit him?

The handle of his bedroom door squeaked, and Harry's heart jumped as if it had been zapped by an electric current. For a moment he hoped a draught had merely rattled the door, but no, the door was opening as he watched. He reached out for the torch and switched it on, then quickly aimed the beam at the opening door.

A strange sight was revealed by the beam of that torch. It looked like a black suit of clothes standing there with a very unreal head – almost like the head of a shop window dummy of the type you see in Burtons and Marks and Spencers. The face had no expression at all, and no clearly defined eyes; they were more like the eyes of a marble statue, with no colour to them, and no visible eyebrows. The clothes seemed to be clad around a torso that seemed almost flat, and the legs were the same, and this surreal aspect of the apparition caused Harry's heart to palpitate. The thing seemed to be held back by the beam of the torch, because when Harry moved that beam away to the left, the entity moved a little further towards the bed, but when the beam was trained back on the figure, it retreated a little.

'Who are you?' Harry cried out, his voice almost

closed up with fear. 'Go away.'

The door behind the odd-looking ghost then opened as if by an invisible hand, and a howling wind whistled through the room which blew the magazine off the bedside cabinet. The ghost flew out of the room and Harry sat up rigidly in the bed, stiff with fear as he heard the rustling of the visitant's attire as it flew down the stairs.

The lights then came back on. Harry then jumped out of his skin when he heard the girl next door scream out at the top of her voice and call for her dad. Harry got dressed as quickly as he could then left the bedroom and turned the light on in the hallway. He crept down the stairs and once again he could hear the distinctive chopping sound out in the back garden. He went down to the hallway, switched on the light there, then turned on the lights in the living room and kitchen. He lifted the net curtains in the kitchen window and cupped his left hand around his left eye as he gazed through the window out into the blackness of the back garden, and there was that weird ghost with the false-looking head and flattish body, going in circles around the table – and the long white-handled axe – which was supposed to be under lock and key in the shed, was being swung at the figure by a black shadowy figure. Harry could just about see the black hands gripping the axe handle. The axe head whacked the head of the ghost several times and it seemed to fall, then get up and run around in circles, around the table and the chopped-up remains of the benches. Harry swore when he saw this, and he thought about going outside to get a better look, but was too afraid to do so. Then the ghost with the head of a manikin came running towards the kitchen window, but stopped for a moment, and it triggered the infra-red passive sensor of the security light, which instantly lit up the garden. Now Harry could see the spine-chilling sight of the axe-wielding ghost. It was a pure silhouette – a walking shadow – and it was swinging the axe at the thing with the window-dummy head. Harry swore, and then he saw the axe come down with quite some force, and its blade embedded itself in the crown of the ghost with the peculiar lifeless head. The silhouetted axeman pulled the axe and dragged the unearthly victim towards him. The victim fell to its knees and the shadowy psychopath placed its foot on the shoulder of its kneeling prey and dragged the axe blade out of its head – only to strike it again and again. Harry ran out of the house and knocked on his neighbour's door. The father of the household answered, and Harry stammered: 'Did-did you see it? Hitting him with the axe?'

The father put his index finger to his lips and then beckoned Harry into the hallway. 'We've just calmed her down,' he whispered, raising his eyes to the ceiling, indicating that he was referring to his hysterical daughter. 'We're getting used to all this now,' the father said.

'What's going on?' Harry asked, confused, then added: 'It came into my room, and all the lights went out.'

'I know,' said the neighbour, 'that happens to everyone who moves into your place. We think there might have been a murder there in the past -

an axe murder, but no one around here seems to remember any such murder.'

Screams were heard again upstairs, and the neighbour said to Harry: 'She's off again. Bear with me a moment, I'll be right back.' And he rushed up the stairs, followed by his wife. Harry couldn't take any more of this. He left his haunted house that night and went to stay with his sister until he managed to put the house up for sale. Harry had to put the house on the market for a ridiculously low price, but was only too glad when he finally moved out to a flat in south Liverpool. No one knows the back story to the haunting. It would seem, from the many accounts I have heard of the ghostly goings-on, that some axe murder took place in the back garden of the house, but surely such an atrocity would have been well known and the newspapers and television news people would have reported it? And yet I have found no reports of any such barbaric murder in Norris Green and I have spent hours going through the newspaper archives of three decades. There is, of course, a possibility that some gruesome murder was committed at that house on Netherwood Road, and that the killer got away with his crime, or, could it even be some timeslip, where we are seeing a future murder that has yet to take place there? It's a real conundrum, and as far as I know, the phantom sounds of the wood-chopper were heard as recently as 2009. Hopefully, we may learn more about this puzzling Norris Green haunting in the near future.

MR HOLT

On the Thursday morning of June 13, 1963, at half-past two, a young black musician named Charles left a party on Stanhope Street in Toxteth and decided to walk home to Kensington. The moon was looming at rooftop level and the stars presented a majestic spectacle in the small hours of this morning. As Charles walked along Hope Street carrying his guitar case, he heard footsteps following, but whenever he stopped, so did the footfalls, so he assumed he was listening to the echoes of his own feet on the pavement – but he was wrong, for as he passed Blackburne House, he heard a low rich-sounding voice over his right shoulder say, 'Hello there.'

Charles turned to see a straight-backed man of about six feet in height with a top hat on. He looked to be around sixty-five, perhaps older. He wore a long black cape and carried a walking cane. Charles could see he was no ghost as he was solid, and the musician had seen the local eccentric 'Sir' Frederick Bowman, who often went about town in a top hat, monocle, and opera cape when it suited him. 'Hiya,' Charles replied, 'that's nice gear; have you been to a party?'

The stranger emitted a high-pitched shriek of a laugh as he tossed back his head – and his hat fell off. He picked it up, put it back on, and said, 'Me? Go to a party? Ha! No, not me lad, I can't rest that's all, damned insomnia! Can't rest at all!'

Charles decided to make no further references to the oddball's quaint attire, and he walked on a few steps before the man said, 'George Holt!' and thrust his hand out. Charles shook it and said, 'Charles,' but never gave a surname. 'And you're a musician?' Holt queried, eyeing the guitar case. Charles nodded and talked about his love of the blues – and then realised he was alone. He looked about the empty silent moonlit street and hurried homewards. That Mr Holt had left the scene awfully quick – too quick in fact, Charles mused.

In December that year, Charles played at a Christmas Eve party at a house on Upper Parliament Street, and ended up leaving at half-past three. As he walked homewards along Hope Street he was set upon by two roughs at the side street of the Philharmonic Hall. They wanted the guitar and the musician's wallet and watch. One of the men had a knife.

There was a shriek of laughter! George Holt came

running down Caledonia Street with his arms in the air and his cloak billowing upwards behind him. He struck the heads and limbs of the would-be muggers with his cane, and seeing how sinister the attacker looked – the two men fled. Then quite calmly, Holt said to a stunned Charles: 'I cannot sleep again. There's rainwater dripping into my tomb; splash, splash, splash! And it's a singular annoyance!'

Charles shuddered at Mr Holt's remark about a 'tomb'. 'You're a ghost – ' Charles muttered, and he ran off, but slipped twice on the snow as he tried to put as much distance as he could between himself and the solid-looking ghost.

'That's a marvellous way to thank me for saving your neck!' cried the ghost, 'What the deuce does it matter if I am a damned ghost? You'll be one yourself soon enough me lad!'

Charles ran off around a corner, and halted for a moment out of breath by the Royal Children's Hospital on Myrtle Street, where he looked back to see the silhouette of Mr Holt standing on the corner. He looked so forlorn and in need of a friend, but Charles ran off into the night, and for the rest of his days he only walked down Hope Street during the hours of daylight.

NIGHT NURSE TALES

Avril is in her late eighties now, but many years ago she was a nurse at a major Liverpool hospital. Here's a strange tale she told me. At 3am one windy October morning in 1959, Avril was sat at her desk, overlooking the darkened ward of thirty male patients. In the still of a morning like this, Avril found her mind wandering through time and space, butterfly fashion, landing on the various flowers of events in her life of 32 years. She ruminated on the ruins of doomed love affairs of the past upon this morning as the wind howled and lifted twirling, tumbling leaves at the ward windows of the hospital. Sometimes Avril wondered how she had come to be sitting there in her white starched cap and crisp uniform. She had originally wanted to be a singer in her younger days, but that dream was lost somewhere along the way. As Avril sat there in her reveries, she thought she heard a man's voice echoing in the distance. What was he saying? He was shouting her name! Avril looked around. Every patient was sleeping, even the regular bed-wetter in bed six. The 20-year-old lad in bed 16 often cried in his sleep, but this was not his high-pitched voice; this was a deep manly voice, but where was it coming from? Avril looked behind her, for that was where she now believed the voice was coming from – and she suddenly saw a semi-transparent face with a blue tint to it appear in the darkness. It was the head of a bald man, aged about thirty-five perhaps, and the face of this apparition wore a broad grin.

'Avril, I don't half fancy you girl – are you with anyone?' said the phantom head, and its voice was clearer and louder now.

Avril was even mindful of the well-being of the patients as she faced the lustful ghost, and although she was scared, she stood her ground and in a low voice, she firmly told the entity to 'Get lost! Go back wherever you came from!'

'Ah, don't be like that love, I only want a kiss and some cuddling, and a nice little feel,' said the phantasm, and the night nurse closed her eyes tightly and made the sign of the cross, then she opened one eye and saw that the salacious spectre was still hovering there, and was now making disgusting, suggestive gestures with his tongue.

Tommy, the lad in bed 16 awoke and asked for Avril, and she went to see what the matter was. 'What's that thing by your desk? What is it?' Tommy asked, excitedly, and Avril was so relieved he could see the ghostly head too, but she assured Tommy it was just one of the porters messing about and shining a torch on his face from under his chin. Tommy doubted this explanation, and became worried at the sight of the glowing head. Avril put a screen between the lad and the ghost, and when she went back to her desk the spectral sex pest had thankfully vanished – but he reappeared to the night nurse at 2 am the next morning and came out with a string of obscene words. The ghost seemed to be bent on taunting the night nurse and she tried to shield her ears from the demonic foul-mouthed head. Avril took to bringing a Bible in to work each night, but a few days later when she was on the day shift, she was put on another ward – and there, laying in a bed on this ward was the unmistakable bald man who had somehow haunted her each night, and he was gazing at her with a knowing look. He had been recovering from a serious operation at the hospital for two weeks, and was discharged that day before Avril could confront and quiz him, but five months later she received a Valentine Card signed "The Ghost". Avril suspected it was from that eerie patient, but was naturally confused as to how he could possibly visit her in the form of a glowing disembodied head. Had that patient been somehow able to project his soul from his body? The occultists call such a dark talent astral projection, and I and many other people have experienced astral projection in the form of out-of-body experiences. These experiences can occur when a person is asleep, unusually stressed, seriously ill, or anesthetized whilst undergoing an operation. The person finds himself floating out his body and is sometimes able to visit any place by the sheer power of thought. Perhaps the phantasm that visited Avril in the wee small hours was the astral body of the man on the downstairs ward who had, perhaps, had a lustful eye for the night nurse.

Shirley is another woman who once worked as a nurse in the old Northern Hospital, which once stood near Old Hall Street in the 1970s. Around 1975, Shirley went on the night shift for a while, and during her stint as a night nurse, she witnessed something very strange. She did her midnight round, tending to the needs of the male patients, cleaning and changing a few of the older men, and she even chatted to a few of the patients when they had difficulty sleeping. Around 1.40 am every patient in the ward was sleeping or settled down for the night, and Shirley sat at her desk with her desk lamp being the only source of illumination in the ward. She looked over her notes on what medication she was to give to the patients at certain times, while outside, rain was pelting the windows of the ward. When the rain shower abated a few minutes later, Shirley became aware of a rustling of fabric behind her, and turned to see a woman with dark curly hair in a long white nightdress walking down the corridor outside (which was visible because one of the double doors to the ward was open). This stranger walked past Shirley in a nonchalant manner, and Shirley said 'Excuse me,' and rose from her desk to go after the inappropriately dressed female, but the woman walked very fast to one bed and she touched the hand of the sleeping man, then bent over the patient and kissed him. Shirley got to within six feet of this audacious woman and witnessed her sudden dematerialisation. 'She was there one moment, then gone,' Shirley recalled the vanishing act when I met her in 2008. Shirley realised that she had seen a ghost, and told no one. The patient the ghostly woman had kissed woke up and asked who had kissed him. Shirley told the man he had been dreaming, but later that day, the two sons of this man visited him in the hospital and broke the tragic news: their mother had passed away from a heart attack this morning at a quarter to two. The patient was naturally heartbroken and during his further stay in the hospital, he showed Shirley a photograph of his late wife, and it was the very woman who had passed the night nurse that morning at the time of her death. She had the same curly dark hair and the same distinctive nose and other facial features. Shirley reasoned that the woman had returned in spirit to kiss her husband goodbye for the last time - on this earth anyway.

SOME HEADLESS GHOSTS

Headless ghosts, such as the purported spectre of Anne Boleyn, may seem like a cliché of the supernatural world, but locally there have been quite a few headless ghosts reported to me over the years. As recently as 2010 the phantom of a headless priest was seen walking past the windows of Blackwell's bookshop on Brownlow Hill. I am convinced that this is the same headless priest who started to haunt that area of the city when the old Arch Diocese building on Brownlow Hill was demolished a few years ago, and I have mentioned this alarming apparition in one of the *Haunted Liverpool* books. Here are a few other accounts of ghosts that have lost their heads for various reasons.

Burtonwood airfield, located just two miles northwest of Warrington, opened on 1 January 1940 as a servicing and storage depot for British planes, run by the RAF's No 37 Maintenance Unit, but as World War Two escalated the base was handed over to the United States Army Air Forces from 1942, although there was still an RAF presence at Burtonwood until about 1943. During the war years, Burtonwood was the largest military airfield in Europe, and was known as Lancashire's Detroit because of the sheer number of planes processed there; between 1943 and 1945, some 11,575 aircraft were processed, and over forty thousand engines were built there. By the end of the war, 18,000 American servicemen were stationed at the airbase which would subsequently play a major role in the Berlin Airlift of 1948. Of course, during the war years, the Yanks, as the Americans were known to most English people, took over the nearby town of Warrington and many of the local females were attracted to what they saw as dashing handsome American servicemen, and many of the local women saw the possibility of escape from the humdrum life of a Lancashire town for the imagined glamour and excitement of a life stateside with an American husband. At this time, Burtonwood airbase had become a bustling community in its own right, a 15-square mile piece of America planted on Lancashire soil. The base had five churches, three cinemas, and a 200-bed hospital with five dentists and eight doctors – and, of course, the base had its own nightclub – the Skyline. The local girls who dreamed of dating the American airmen had to provide two letters of recommendation to gain entry into the club, as well as undergoing a lengthy interview with a US welfare officer. The club was a hit with the

Lancashire lasses and special bus routes were put on to take the girls to the club. Almost 7,000 American servicemen married the local girls of Liverpool, Warrington and Newton-le-Willows during these years, and around 1942, a 24-year-old Liverpool woman, named Lilian is said to have been about to marry a Texan pilot when he met a ghastly fate at the base. It was said that during the period when the film actor James Stewart (who was then the pilot of a B24 Liberation bomber) visited the base, a pilot accidentally walked into the engine propeller of a plane and was instantly decapitated. The headless body allegedly ran a few yards (as guillotined bodies in the French Revolution occasionally did) then collapsed before horrified onlookers. Lilian wasn't told of the dreadful accident and turned up at the base a few nights later looking for her fiancé, and no one had the heart to tell her about his grisly fate. Lilian left the Skyline club and wandered out onto a nearby moonlit field where she saw a familiar figure approach in the distance. From the way the figure walked she knew it was her boyfriend, but then she saw he had no head, and fainted. Several other witnesses including three airmen said they saw the headless apparition pick up the unconscious Lilian and embrace her as it seemed to dance. The full moon slid behind a cloud and when it re-emerged seconds later the headless ghostly airman was gone, but he then began to haunt the base and although Burtonwood has now been demolished, it is said that the headless airman still haunts the place where the base once stood.

One sunny afternoon in June 2004, two students

in their early twenties went to get a "smoothie" (a healthy drink made of liquefied and blended fruits) at a stall in Clayton Square. As the girls waited for their drinks at the stall, one of them noticed a figure coming down a nearby escalator: it was a smartly dressed man in a light beige sportscoat, black jeans and a pair of expensive-looking shoes. This man had no head, and when the student quickly noticed this she almost fainted. She drew her friend's attention to the headless figure, and so there were now two witnesses to this inexplicable entity. There then came a few screams and a middle-aged woman is said to have collapsed upon seeing the headless ghost walk towards her. I received many emails and phone calls about the so-called headless man of Clayton Square shopping centre, including a detailed account from a teenage brother and sister who were coming out of the Paper Mill shop when they almost collided with the grisly apparition. The figure was solid enough to make a tapping noise as its shoes strode towards the Church Street exit of the shopping centre. And then, as the figure approached a florist, it vanished. As far as I know, the headless entity has not been seen since at Clayton Square and no one knows whose headless ghost walked that day or why. So many people from all walks of life saw the apparition, that I do not believe a hoaxer was at work, but I am at a loss to explain this fascinating but scary ghost, which is something of a rarity, because it was seen not in poor lighting, but in the hours of broad daylight in a well-lit shopping centre.

Many years ago in the 1950s, two Liverpool

schoolgirls – Susan, age 13 and Ann, aged 14, spent the summer school holidays in Shrewsbury at the house of Ann's Aunt Connie. On the first night at Connie's house, Susan had a gruesome nightmare and woke the house up with her screams. In the dream, Susan was hiding behind a sofa upon which Ann was sitting reading, and intended to scare her by jumping up and grabbing her head, but when she did this in the dream, Ann's head came away in her hands, and Susan looked at it in shock. Ann's eyes were closed and her mouth was wide open and her tongue was dangling from the limp jaw. At that point, Susan awakened in a state of terror because the dream had been so realistic, she had vividly felt Ann's silky bob of hair and even felt her dangling tongue tip on her wrist. Connie burst into the room to calm Susan down and eventually convinced her that she had suffered nothing more than a bad dream.

On the following day, the two girls went to a local fairground, where they went on the waltzers, the Ferris wheel and various other rides. Ann wanted to go on the Helter Skelter, but Susan wanted to go and get some candy floss first. Ann stormed off in a huff, saying they could have some later, and tried to take a short cut to the Helter Skelter by climbing a rail which enclosed part of a big dipper. Somehow she slipped as she climbed over the rail and landed with her head stuck between the railings. At this point the big dipper train of carriages (known as a roller coaster in the US) came thundering down and smashed into the trapped girl's legs, throwing her body forward – but because her head was trapped between the railings, the girl was decapitated, and the impact sent the head of Ann rolling across the fairground until it came to a halt by hitting Susan's right ankle as she stood at a van buying candy floss. At first the girl thought someone had kicked a football at her, and she looked down – and saw Ann's severed head, spurting blood from the stump of her neck. Ann's mouth was opening and closing as she bit at the grass, and then, just before Susan fainted, she saw the tongue of the still-living head flop out of the mouth and onto the grass. Bystanders said the eyes of the severed head stared at them in terror for a few moments, and then rolled backwards.

As you can imagine, Susan bore deep mental scars because of this grisly, traumatic incident, and when she said she was being stalked by Ann's headless body after she returned to Liverpool, people assumed that her mind had merely been unhinged by witnessing the horrific death of her friend – but then other people began to see the solid-looking headless ghost in the school Ann attended in Liverpool, and one of these witnesses was a teacher at the school, who saw the headless schoolgirl walking down a corridor towards him with her blazer and shirt soaked with blood. The witness, a man who taught history, was in his fifties and had no interest in the supernatural, but was left badly shaken by the encounter. When he saw Ann's ghost coming towards him he had to open a fire exit door to get out of the building. It is said that a priest from St Anthony's finally confronted the ghost and it never returned after it had been 'counselled'.

Susan died in the 1980s and periodically relived the horrific fairground accident in nightmares for decades. She was convinced that the nightmare of Ann losing her head was some type of warning which unfortunately she and her friend did not heed.

THE VANISHED

After reading the uncanny story in the chapter entitled "Libra" in *Haunted Liverpool 10*, which detailed the intentions of a pointy-headed entity to abduct two children at Irby Heath, Wirral, in 1973, a West Derby woman named Maria Sownessy got in touch with me to tell me how she had a similar encounter with a would-be abductor in 1969.

On Tuesday 8 April, 1969, Maria Sownessy celebrated her 13th birthday, and one of the gifts she received was a beautiful silver girl's bike, which she pedalled straight out of her home in Wharncliffe Road, Old Swan. Maria was warned by her mother Doris to watch out for traffic, and Maria shouted, 'I will!' in reply as she set off for her friend Tina's house on North Drive, Sandfield Park, about half a mile away to the north. It was around 6.10pm when Maria reached Tina's house, and Tina got her old bike out and the two teenagers went on a cycling trip round Stoneycroft and then onto West Derby Village. Around 8.40pm, the sun had set and twilight was falling quickly, so Maria decided it was time she went home, and she invited Tina to come back to her house with her to have some birthday cake. Tina said she knew a shortcut to her friend's home, but she got mixed up with one of the roads and took a wrong turn which took her and Maria near Yew Tree Lane, close to West Derby Golf Course. Meanwhile, back at Maria's house on Wharncliffe Road, her mother Doris said she had a bad feeling about Maria being out so late and asked her husband Graham to go and look for her, but he said she'd be home soon and remained seated in front of the TV watching *Life With Cooper* – which featured the legendary comedian Tommy Cooper – and Graham was enjoying the programme as he sipped a glass of whiskey.

Around this time, as Maria's mum was having some sort of premonition about her daughter, Maria was peddling her bike down Honey's Green Lane (where Cardinal Heenan High School now stands) when Maria noticed a man standing in the middle of the road ahead. It was impossible not to have noticed this individual because he was a peculiar-looking man of unusual height – apparently about 7 feet or more – and he was dressed in a one-piece suit which looked pea green in colour. But the weird thing that really stood out from this abnormally tall man was the strange pointed hat he wore. It was reminiscent of a wizard or witch's archetypal hat, only it had no rim. 'Ha! Look at him!' Tina shouted as she caught up with Maria on her bike, and at this point Maria sensed there was something menacing about the giant in the pointed hat. She slowed down and tried to steer the bike around him, and Tina's bike followed her friend's curved path, and both girls recalled that at this point, all of the sounds of the traffic in the distance seemed to stop. 'Who is he?' Tina asked with a smile, and looked back as she saw the man beckon her with his hand.

'Don't look back! Keep going Tina!' Maria advised, and felt butterflies in her stomach.

Both girls then felt something tugging at their bikes. Tina later said it was as if someone had attached a long elastic rope to the back of the bike and tied the other end to a tree. Both girls pedalled furiously but they felt something – some sinister force – dragging their bikes back – and back towards the man with the pointy hat. Tina lifted her backside off the seat of her bike and pressed down with her weight into the pedals – and the gear-chain came off. Tina then jumped off the bike as it shot backwards as if it was being attracted to some giant scrap-yard electromagnet. Maria squeezed the brake levers on the handlebars and let out a yelp when she felt her brand new bike being dragged along by the mysterious force – towards the most bizarre figure she had ever seen. Then she noticed that the man in the pea green one-piece suit and conical hat was walking towards her. She heard him say: "You're a case', in a thick Scouse accent, but when she heard him say this phrase again, parrot fashion, she was near enough to see that the entity's mouth was not moving and that the sounds of its speech were coming from some sort of loudspeaker in the chest area of the figure – as if it was a recording. At closer quarters, Tina could see that the face of the tall lanky man was very pale, and his eyes had no white to them – they were just black eyeballs and the irises looked silvery, but Tina is not sure of this because of the dim street lighting on that stretch of road. She did also note that the man's nose was aquiline and quite large, and his chin was pointed. She cannot remember if the clothing he wore had buttons or zippers. Maria saw at close quarters that the pointy hat the weird-looking man wore seemed to be part of some balaclava which covered the sides of the head but allowed the ears – which were long and prominent – to stick out. She also noticed that the green one piece suit had a collar that covered the entity's entire neck up to his jaw, and that he wore no gloves, but had boots similar to Wellingtons that were also pea green in colour. Maria also thought she detected a disagreeable odour around this figure which reminded her of ammonia.

Maria ran off, dragging Tina with her with such force, the latter fell over and Maria had to pick her up and the two girls fled the scene in absolute terror. They told a man walking his dog on Eaton Road about the strangely-dressed figure but he just smiled as if he thought the girls were pulling his leg, so they ran on through the gathering dusk and never stopped running until they reached Maria's home on Wharncliffe Road, where Maria's mother Doris was waiting on the doorstep. She looked so relieved when she saw her daughter all out of breath coming towards her, but then Doris saw she had tears in her eyes, and she asked her where her bike was and where she'd been. Maria and her best friend went into the kitchen and excitedly told of their extramundane experience. Doris told her husband Graham what had happened and he found the story very far-fetched, and yet he had never known his daughter to tell lies. He went to Honey's Green Lane with his younger brother Bert who lived in the next street, and the two men found Tina's bike laying on the pavement, but there was no sign of Maria's brand-new bike anywhere. Then Bert spotted the missing bike on nearby Blackmoor Drive. A child of about 9 was riding it with another child sitting on the seat with him (having a "takey" as we used to say). Bert challenged the boys and they dropped the bike and ran off.

There was no sign of any 7-foot-tall man in green with a conical hat, and after Graham and Bert had dropped the recovered bikes off at the house on Wharncliffe Road, they both went to the pub.

That night, around half-past twelve, Maria lay in bed, thinking about the sinister figure she and Tina had seen on Honey's Green Lane, and after the girl's mother had come up to tuck her daughter in - and to also reassure her that the strange man she had seen had been some oddball prankster – Maria fell into an uneasy sleep. She woke around three in the morning – and saw a terrifying shadow cast on the closed curtains of her room: it was a triangular shadow – just like the shape of the head of the giant who had somehow pulled Maria and Tina's bikes towards him. Maria shouted her mother and father at the top of her voice, and the shadow on the curtain flitted away. When Doris and a bleary-eyed Graham barged into their daughter's bedroom, they found Maria cowering under the blankets. Doris believed her daughter had genuinely encountered something not of this earth, but Graham believed she had merely experienced a realistic nightmare. Thankfully, Maria and Tina never saw the figure with the bizarre cone-shaped hat again, but many years later, Maria read an account of a figure matching the exact description of the entity she and her friend saw in the tenth volume of the *Haunted Liverpool* series, and she went cold. In that book I told the story related to me of a strange being with a pointed head and strange green attire who tried to lure two children into a craft that resembled a giant indigo-coloured toadstool. The abduction attempt, by the weird unnaturally tall entity, was unsuccessful, but a month later, the national press reported that a boy and girl on the Isle of Wight had been confronted with a very strange figure which matched the one seen in 1969 by Maria and Tina. He too wore steeple-shaped headgear of some sort and was dressed in a one-piece green suit. The children on the Isle of Wight asked the weird humanoid if he was a ghost, and in a strange voice he gave a rather ambiguous reply: 'Well, not really, but I am in an odd sort of way,' he told them, and when the youngsters asked him what he meant by this, all he would say was: 'You know.'

Luckily for the children on the Isle of Wight, the towering odd figure gave up enticing them into a bizarre-looking dwelling - which resembled a toadstool in shape – and he, and his peculiar 'house' subsequently vanished.

It may be a dark coincidence, but on the very day Maria and Tina ran into the 7-foot man on Honey's Green Lane, a 13-year-old girl named April Fabb vanished under very strange circumstances in Norfolk. At around 1.40pm on the Tuesday afternoon of 8 April 1969, the teenager left her home in Metton, near Cromer in Norfolk, on her bike, bound for her married sister's house in Roughton, just two miles away, but at 2.15pm that afternoon, two Ordnance Survey workers found April's blue and white bicycle dumped behind a hedge just a mile from her home, and there was no sign of the girl anywhere. Despite an intensive search by 120 police, airmen and frogmen, no clue to the whereabouts of the missing teenager was found, and to this day, no one knows what happened to April Fabb. It transpired that the girl had met her fate around nine minutes after she had left home, and this would have been at a spot that was well within earshot of picnickers, and yet no one saw or heard anything, which deepens this mystery; it was as if something had just come down and taken April, leaving only her bicycle behind. Detective-Chief-superintendent Lester of the Norfolk CID was drafted in to deal with the baffling disappearance and he told the Press: 'We are treating April's disappearance extremely seriously. She is a happy home-loving girl and there is no reason why she would want to leave home.'

April's 52-year-old father Ernest also told journalists: 'April is not the sort of girl to just vanish. If she had decided to go off, surely she wouldn't have dumped her bicycle.'

The parents waited, hoping to hear some news or some scrap of evidence to explain the weird vanishing act, but nothing more was ever heard of April Fabb since that Tuesday afternoon in April 1969. I am probably way off the mark, and in all probability, April was tragically murdered and her body was subsequently disposed by some person or persons unknown, possibly after a sexual assault, but the date of her disappearance stuck out in my mind because a paranormal would-be abductor from God knows where (and when) was encountered by two girls who were aged 13 – just like April, and they, like April, had been on a bike at the time. There's another strange twist to this conjecture; nine years after the disappearance of April Fabb, another 13-year-old vanished while riding a bike, and this teenager has never been seen since either. I am referring to the enigmatic disappearance of Genette Tate on 19 August 1978. Acting Detective-Chief-Superintendent Eric Rundle, deputy head of Cornwall and Devon police, was one of the first people to notice the chilling similarities between the disappearance of Tate and Fabb, but this comparison yielded nothing to throw any light on the disappearance of Genette Tate. Genette left her home in the village of Aylesbeare, Devon, on the sunny Saturday afternoon of 19 August 1978, and went to a nearby pub to collect the bundle of newspapers she had to deliver (mostly to farms in the area). At 3.30pm, Genette put the newspapers in her satchel and then rode off to start her delivery round on her blue Chopper bike. Genette was only doing this newspaper delivery job to fill in for the regular paperboy who was on holiday. Around four o'clock that sunny Saturday afternoon, Genette met two friends named Margaret and Tracey, and stopped for a while to chat to them, and then Genette said she'd better get on with her deliveries and rode off up the lane and turned a corner, vanishing from sight. Margaret and Tracey walked on, heading in the same direction towards that corner. This lane was known as Within Lane, a narrow tree-lined track which has an expanse of fields on either side of it. Well, as Margaret and Tracey turned the corner, they saw Genette's blue Chopper bike lying on its side, and the satchel of newspapers had been discarded nearby and some of the newspaper were scattered about. There was no sign of Genette Tate anywhere, but the girls scanned the fields left and right, and could see no one. The girls called Genette's name out loud but no reply came. The Genette Tate case is still the longest missing persons inquiry in British history. In the short time it had taken for Margaret and Tracey to reach the corner Genette had turned on her Chopper bike about 8-10 minutes earlier, someone had snatched the girl and whisked her away, even though no one in the area saw anyone about. The two girls heard no car or van driving off around that corner, and they definitely did not hear any screams or voices – so what the devil happened to Genette? The *Guardian* newspaper gave an accurate summing up of the mystery a week after the disappearance: 'Police are facing one of the most puzzling disappearances on record. No evidence has been found. No fact uncovered to suggest what might have happened to Genette.'

Over 150 police, supplemented by hundreds of neighbours, went in search of the missing schoolgirl, and a helicopter from RAF Chivenor was also used in the search – all to no avail. John Anderson, Chief Constable of Devon and Cornwall, admitted the case was a complete mystery. Bloodhounds, thousands of volunteers, mediums and a hypnotist were enlisted in the extended search for Genette, but there was no breakthrough. At one point, a mother and daughter reported seeing a maroon Triumph 1300 saloon speeding along the lane where Genette's bike had been found, and the witnesses even provided police with a part of the vehicle's registration, but all this came to nothing. Eventually, Detective Chief Inspector Eric Rundle, who led the investigation, admitted: 'Our local inquiries have petered out.'

An inch-by-inch survey of Within Lane uncovered no forensic indications of what happened that sunny Saturday afternoon, and the case may never be solved – unless there is a deathbed confession by someone or perhaps if Genette's DNA can be found in a place it shouldn't be – for in 2002, a useful sample of the missing girl's DNA was lifted from a jumper Genette had once worn, now treasured by her mother Sheila.

The transcendent truth behind some inexplicable disappearances of the type detailed here may never be known, unless of course you, the reader happen to one day find yourself walking into Limbo or being confronted with some being from another time or dimension who regards you as something to be collected. I have interviewed many people who almost vanished into obscurity, and if we are to believe their accounts, we are open to a powerful and inexplicable force at large that can abduct us at any time and any place. In August 2004, two women in their twenties, named Neeley and Alice, left a branch of HMV on Liverpool's Church Street, and went next door to Next, and as they walked through the doors to this store, Neeley experienced something which she could only describe as a "funny turn"; she felt as if something was drawing her upwards, and became quite dizzy, but she quickly recovered from this spell of giddiness. About twenty minutes afterwards, Alice suggested going to Cavern Walks, and so they walked up Church Street, through "Holy Corner" (where holy-themed Whitechapel, Paradise, Church and Lord Street meet), and then went down Doran's Lane, a narrow alleyway leading to Harrington Street which has an entrance next to British Home Stores. Halfway down Doran's Lane, Neeley had another dizzy spell and felt herself again being drawn up. She likened the sensation to what she imagined would happen if someone wearing a steel helmet stood under a scrap-yard magnet. This time she blacked out after seeing a bright light, as bright as a laser, shining in her eyes from just above eye level. At this point, Alice suddenly noticed that Neeley was nowhere to be seen in Doran's Lane – she had literally been walking alongside Alice one moment and then Alice had heard the rhythmic sound of her friend's flip-flops suddenly cease. A dishevelled-looking man who often begged in that area of the city had been sitting a few feet away, and he was gawping at the space besides Alice where Neeley had been walking seconds ago. As Alice looked about frantically, the beggar remained open-mouthed and wide-eyed – as if he had seen the girl disappear into thin air. Alice looked about and saw three shoppers walking towards her from Harrington Street, and just after they passed, the beggar swore out loud and Alice looked over at him. He was pointing at something behind her. Neeley had returned, and she was leaning against a wall with a dazed expression. She had no recollection of where she had been, and seemed a bit disoriented. For a few moments the girl seemed to suffer from amnesia, and did not recognise Alice, and then it all came back. She remembered the feeling of being pulled upwards, of warmness on the top of her head and the nape of her neck as she was blinded by a strange light – but everything after that until the moment when Alice found her was a blank. Neeley was so afraid of this experience she never ventured anywhere near Doran's Lane and Lord Street for years. She also began to have a series of strange distinctive dreams in which she was in a huge white-tiled hall. She always felt at home in this hall whenever she dreamt about it, but once she had awakened she wouldn't have a clue where the place was.

Had something – some higher intelligent force of some kind, attempted to snatch Neeley for some unknown reason, only to return her because, perhaps, she never met the requirements of the abductor? I tracked down the beggar who had been in Doran's Lane and quizzed him about that afternoon, and he described Alice and Neeley accurately, and told me that, 'the blonde one [Neeley] went see-through, like a ghost, and then [clicking his fingers] – gone! And then about twenty seconds – if it was even that – she was back again. It was really trippy.'

A PAIR OF BLUE EYES

The time was precisely 3.30am on a freezing January morning in 1899, when a common thief crept up the black-iced back alleys of Renshaw Street. The street was deserted, except for a solitary caped policeman on his lonely beat along the deadly quiet thoroughfare. As the sentinel stars shone down on that crystal-clear moonless night, the bobby continued past the old Adelphi Hotel and turned up Copperas Hill, unaware that the sharp eyes of a consummately clever thief were watching his every step.

Silent as a ghost, the nocturnal criminal, fifty-six-year-old Henry Swann of Moon Street (near Pembroke Place), surveyed the immediate area once again, before closing in on the pillar box. Swann produced a leaden weight smeared with sticky bird-lime from an old metal cigar tube. Attached to the weight was a five foot length of fishing line. The modus operandi of Mr Swann was to fish for letters in the pillar box with the sticky weight. He had had some sizeable returns from his 'angling' as he called it. Even today, people often send money through the post (usually by way of recorded delivery), and in the days of Henry Swann, it was a common occurrence to send banknotes, coins, jewellery and other valuable items through the efficient and trusted postal system.

Swann tugged the line, and sensed he had a catch. He reeled it up and manipulated the cushy envelope through the mouth of the pillar box. Three more letters were extracted before Swann decided to quit while he was ahead. He had pushed his luck on the previous night and had almost been seen by a lamplighter, so he quickly shut down his nefarious operation. He thought he heard a voice and froze like a startled rodent, but was soon relieved when he realised that it was the snoring of some noisy sleeper in Heathfield Street who had left his bedroom window slightly ajar. Soon the policeman would be round again on his clockwork patrol, so Swann deposited the gummy weight in the cigar container and wound the twine around its cylinder. Up Leece Street he moved stealthily homewards, with the four envelopes tucked snugly against his belly under his belted coat.

Moon Street once ran from Crown Street, until, like the many old streets of Edge Hill, it was levelled in the 1960s to make way for the sprawling campus of Liverpool University. At a dingy terraced house on Moon Street in 1899, Henry Swann lived with his nine-year-old nephew, Edwin Quinby, who was an orphan. Upon that frigid January morning, Mr Swann entered his home, bolted the door and checked that the curtains were drawn. He lit a candle from the flickering flames in the grate, then positioned it on the table. With relish, he laid the envelopes out ready for inspection. Swann was just in the middle of poking the sealed flap of the first one with an old oyster knife, when the door of the parlour steadily opened. Swann's heart almost stopped with fright. It was young Edwin, unable to sleep because of the relentless, permeating arctic cold.

"I'm freezin' uncle," Edwin sniffled and walked eagerly to the remains of the coal fire with a fuzzy woollen blanket cocooned around him.

"I'll knock your friggin' 'ead off next time you barge in like that," Swann warned the boy, then resumed his lucky dip with the envelopes.

The first one contained a three-page letter composed in illegible, spidery handwriting. It was tossed into the fire, and Edwin gleefully rubbed his hands as he watched the letter curl and shrivel in the flames.

The second envelope was opened. Again there was nothing of any value, only a love letter of florid prose and feverish ramblings penned and signed by a 'Mr X' and addressed to a Miss Elizabeth Paine of 75 Bedford Street. This missive was also delivered into the grate. Edwin, who loved fire, picked up the flaming envelope and letter with a pair of tongs and watched it burn away to carbon flakes.

The third envelope contained a skilfully-executed begging letter, written by a man whom Swann knew well - William Cooke of Sandon Street. Cooke, a failed alcoholic solicitor, had syndicates of begging-letter writers who used his 'templates', as he called them, to extract substantial sums of money from the soft-hearted and the plain gullible. The letters, signed by various names and bearing different return addresses, were targeted at people on a list of known philanthropists. This was one begging letter which would surely go unanswered. Swann crumpled the sham epistle into a ball and hurled it accurately into the fire.

The fourth envelope - a rather padded one at that - was opened. Henry Swann prayed for some sizeable return from his fishing trip. It was a piece of muslin cloth. He pulled it out of the envelope and unwrapped what looked at first like a scarf, but it was soon apparent that it was not. The material swathed a letter - and something so awful that it caused Swann to recoil loudly in terror and disgust. In his hand sat a pair of human eyes!

Edwin dropped the tongs with fright as his uncle yelped and recoiled from the grisly package. Swann hurled himself backwards from the table, scraping the rickety-legged chair across the bare stone floor with a screech.

"What's the matter uncle?" enquired the trembling lad, as he rose from the fireside chair.

Swann was speechless. His eyes were transfixed by the lifeless staring blue irises on the table. Those slimy white disks were actually someone's eyes. They had belonged to a real person who was now blind or dead, Swann reasoned, as he broke out in a clammy sweat.

Edwin edged cautiously towards the table, trying to determine what the strange circular convex white disks were.

"Stay put! Stay there!" Swann bawled, and his nephew obeyed.

"What are they uncle?"

"Eyes," Swann replied, gripping the back of the chair, "they're eyes."

The repulsive objects of fear were the sliced-off frontal sections of human eyeballs, but who had cut them off? A murderer most likely, Swann conjectured. He had to go to the police to tell them about the appalling discovery; but he would have to pretend that he found the envelope on the pavement on Renshaw Street. If the police did not believe him, he would be in real trouble. Also, how could he explain the smears of bird-lime on the envelope? Worse still, Swann pondered on the possibility of being implicated in a possible murder. He regretted fishing at the pillar box in Renshaw Street. Why had he not he tried the pillar box on Brownlow Hill? Because he had seen an annoying fat policeman on point duty earlier that night; that was the reason, Swann recalled.

"Whose eyes are they?" Edwin asked, hiding in his blanket as he stood behind his confused uncle.

"I don't know," Swann admitted. He leaned forward and quickly snatched the leaf of notepaper that had been mailed with the hideous staring eyes. His hand shook with a nervous tremor as Henry Swann whispered out the words of the note:

Dear Mr Appleyard,

I enclose a pair of eyes taken from your daughter's suitor. The rest of him shall follow soon.

Yours faithfully,

A madman who is watching your home.

The disturbing communication confirmed Swann's darkest suspicions; that he had unwittingly embroiled himself in a murder, and a particularly nasty one at that. Perhaps if he simply burned the letter and the eyes, it would be the end of the grave entanglement, but would that not be a crime? Destroying evidence of a murder? Swann had to do something fast before dawn. He considered sending Edwin to the police with the murderer's letter! But Edwin was a dullard who spoke after he thought, so he was sure to slip up and probably even tell the police all about his pillar box fishing expeditions.

Swann anxiously paced back and forth, repeatedly colliding with his nephew, who was following him like a young chick. He suddenly halted and lapsed into a brown study as he looked into the flames. He pictured himself passing the police station, dropping the accursed letter on the pavement under the blue lamp before scuttling off into the night. He quickly dismissed the idea. The very thought of walking in close proximity to a police station, carrying human eyes in an envelope, gave him butterflies in his stomach.

Then an idea surfaced from his subconscious.

Fighting back fear and nausea, he carefully scooped the rubbery eye cross-sections up with the end of the killer's letter, then placed the notepaper and the sliced organs on the muslin cloth. He wrapped the muslin cloth around the letter and the eyes and, with a shudder, shoved the bundle back into the envelope. He sealed the flap with wax from the candle, then turned to Edwin and stooped so that he was at eye level with the docile boy.

"Listen carefully. Take this letter, and go straight to the pillar box in Abercromby Square. Post it, and come straight back. If you see a bobby, and he doesn't see you, come back home. If a bobby stops you and asks you what you've got, tell him that a stranger gave the envelope to you. Have you got all that?"

Edwin nodded doubtfully, and beheld the envelope with a look of horror.

At 4.30am, Edwin Quinby embarked on the short journey from Moon Street to Abercromby Square. Flecks of snow whirled down as the ink-black starry skies clouded over, and Edwin squinted as he paced quickly down Bedford Street through the biting north wind. The streets gradually took on a ghostly appearance as the powdery, wind-driven snow dusted their buildings, lending a spectral aspect to the architecture.

As Edwin was crossing Chestnut Street, he heard a voice. Through the wrought iron railings of a house he caught a fleeting glimpse of a bearded, scruffily-dressed man who was sitting on the steps leading down to a basement door. Edwin panicked. He started to lose his footing as he tried to run over the snow-covered cobbles of the road. The man, who seemed to be a vagrant, shouted something unintelligible and gave chase. Edwin slipped during the chase near the corner of Abercromby Square and grazed his kneecap. The beginnings of a blizzard commenced as the man towered over the fallen boy.

"Give me that!" he growled menacingly and reached for the parcel.

Edwin backed away slightly. A glimmering light caught his attention further up Oxford Street. It was the bull's eye lantern of an approaching policeman.

"A bobby's coming!" Edwin shouted in an optimistic tone, and pointed at the constable, who was now blowing his whistle.

The vagrant twisted round, eyed the policeman, then ran off up Bedford Street. The officer of the law gave chase for a while but soon gave up and ran back towards Edwin.

"What are you doing out on the streets at this unearthly hour?" he asked Edwin, who began to mumble and stutter.

The wax seal on the envelope had broken when he fell, and the policeman picked up the envelope and examined it suspiciously.

That morning at 5.15am, detectives and policemen hammered on the door of Henry Swann's home in Moon Street. Mr Swann knew that he should not have trusted Edwin with such a straightforward, yet important, task, and he cursed the boy as he ran into the back kitchen. Two more policemen hammered on the backyard door. It was no use. Swann opened the front door and he was instantly apprehended.

The house was searched as two detectives questioned him about the letter. Swann immediately confessed to the pillar box theft but denied any involvement in the murder. A policeman soon discovered the cigar tube and the leaden weight coated with quicklime. Swann's house was searched from top to bottom, and the police then took him to the bridewell off Dale Street, where he was interrogated. By noon, Swann was released, and, due to his co-operation in helping to solve a more serious crime, received nothing more than a remarkably generous caution for the serious offence of theft from the Royal Mail pillar boxes.

Swann enquired if the police had managed to discover the identity of the murderer who had sent the repulsive eyes to Mr Appleyard. And, although he was under no obligation to do so, the detective decided to explain the background of the sinister letter.

Since November 1898, James W Appleyard, a music teacher of Catherine Street, had been receiving a stream of poison pen letters, as well as a variety of shocking items delivered by post to his home, including a dead rat, faeces, and other vile and disturbing items. Two of the letters bore Chester franking marks, but the rest had been posted in central Liverpool. Through a strange twist of fate, Mr Swann had unknowingly provided the police with a possible clue to the identity of the lunatic posting the letters and parcels to Mr Appleyard, when the letter containing the eyes had been intercepted in Renshaw Street.

A detective on the case had long held a theory that the man posting the distressing items had been a medical student who had briefly dated Mr Appleyard's daughter, Clara, the previous year. The student in question was discovered to be an opium addict, and so Mr Appleyard forced his daughter to break off her romance with him. Some time later, Clara became engaged to a shipping clerk.

Not long afterwards, the hate mail began to arrive. The spiteful medical student was lodging at the Rotunda Buildings, Rotunda Place, off Bold Street, within a short distance of the pillar box where the eyes had been posted to Mr Appleyard. The eyes contained traces of the kinds of spirits used to preserve medical specimens, and despite the letter's claims, the eyes of Clara's suitor were still intact. Her fiance - Mr Blackwood - was in the best of health in Edinburgh, where he was conducting business.

However, concrete evidence which would prove that the medical student was behind the campaign of postal terror was still lacking, so detectives paid the trainee surgeon a visit. The young man was evidently surprised and apprehensive when detectives quizzed him and searched his digs. Although no evidence was forthcoming, Mr Appleyard never again received any obnoxious letters or parcels - and Henry Swann never went fishing in pillar boxes again.

ST MARK'S EVE

One sunny afternoon around 4.30pm on Thursday 24 April 1980, Philip and Gregory, two 11-year-old boys living in the Wavertree area of Liverpool, went sneaking about in the alleyways off Church Road, opposite the eminent bi-lateral Bluecoat School. Today it was Greg's 11th birthday, and one of the gifts he had received was a so-called 'toy' called Sonic Ear, a device that enabled Greg to listen-in to conversations up to a hundred yards away. Sonic Ear resembled an air rifle in length and shape, and at the end of the gadget's barrel there was a red concave dish, identical in shape to today's satellite dishes – which focused sounds and voices onto a sensitive microphone mounted in the centre of the dish. The signals from this electronic eavesdropping element were then boosted through an amplifier and Greg could hear the amplified results through a type of stethoscope attached to the listening device. Philip had convinced Greg to sneak down the alleyway of Beverley Road and train the dish of the Sonic Ear on the bedroom window of Tracy, a 16-year-old girl both lads had a crush on. Well, when the would-be spies reached the backyard door of Tracy's house, they looked up at her window from the cobbled alleyway and saw to their dismay that the bedroom window of the beautiful teen was closed. Determined to snoop in on any conversation Tracy might be having, Philip pointed out the ventilation grill just to the right of the upper bedroom window, and told Greg to point the listening device at it. Greg switched on the Sonic Ear and did this, and incredibly, he could hear music and faint voices. 'I think she's got a radio on and she's talking to someone,' Greg told his nosy pal as he tried to keep the Sonic Ear aimed firmly at the grill. 'Played! Let's have a listen – go on!' Philip asked with great eagerness, and tried to grab at the stethoscopic hearing tubes planted in Greg's ears, but his friend backed away, saying, 'Shut up!'

Greg squinted slightly as he concentrated on what was being said, but the radio kept drowning out the few words that were being spoken by the girl. When the music died down, the irritating Radio 1 DJ Steve Wright began to talk. 'Oh this is boring,' Greg decided, and walked off. 'Can I have a go? Please,' Philip begged but Greg kept saying 'In a minute, I haven't had a proper go myself yet.'

Philip produced a Jacob's Club Wafer bar and said, 'If you let me have a go you can have this,' and Greg thought about the proposition for a moment then said, 'Nah, I've had loads of birthday cake and me auntie got me a box of Terry's Moonlight chocolates, so I don't want it.'

Eventually Greg gave Philip a go of the Sonic Ear and Philip stuck the hearing tubes of the device in his ears and aimed it up at a jet that was passing overhead. He could hear the amplified rumble of the plane's engines. Then he pointed it at a man and a woman chatting near the mouth of an alleyway on Beverley Road, and Philip grinned widely as he could hear everything the couple were saying. The woman, who looked to be in her fifties, was talking about someone who'd had a hysterectomy. Then Greg started asking for the Sonic Ear back, and Philip said, 'Hey, I can hear something dead loud. Just hang on a minute, honest – I can hear something like a machine over there,' and he pointed to a brick wall.

Greg grappled with his friend and managed to get the toy back, and he listened to the sound Philip had mentioned, and he was right – there was something giving off a strange mechanical, rhythmical sound, and whatever it was it was generating a loud grinding and creaking noise. The lads went up an alleyway, with Greg leading the way as he tried to find the source of the baffling sound. He heard what sounded like bumpkins talking and shouting, and as he tried to make out what they were saying, he heard a blood-curdling scream – a female shriek. Greg jumped and Philip, seeing his friend recoil in fright at whatever he was listening to, asked what he had heard. A woman was screaming and shouting hysterically, and Greg heard her say the word "daughter" distinctly several times.

Then the voices ceased, and all Greg could hear

was the amplified sound of the odd breeze and the magnified hubbub of the traffic on the nearby main roads. The lads went to Greg's house and the latter's mum treated Phil to a teatime meal and a slice of cake. Greg even gave his mate some of his Terry's Moonlight chocolates. Greg mentioned what he had heard to his father, but he took hardly any notice as he watched the telly. Greg's grandfather Joe, however, was intrigued by the account of the ghostly voices and the screaming woman, and he told the boys a strange thing. Joe said that way back, in Victorian times, a huge windmill had stood near Beverley Road. 'If you know where to look, you can still see the foundations of this windmill, like,' Joe told the lads. 'It was called the Crown Mill, and I remember my mother – and she was Wavertree born and bred as I am, like – telling me that when she was a girl, a woman was walking by the Crown Mill when one of the big sails came down and struck her head, and not only that, the poor woman's hair got tangled up in the laths of the sail, and when the sail of the mill went up – you know like, as it turned around – the sail tore her hair, and her scalp clean off. Scalped her like.'

Now Greg's father was listening, and he smiled uneasily and said: 'Scalped? You mean like you see when the Indians scalp cowboys in the cowie films? No bleedin' way.'

'As true as God's in heaven,' Joe told his son-in-law, 'its been written about in one of those Wavertree history books, and my mother wouldn't lie about something like that.'

This little grisly anecdote of granddad's engaged

the imagination of Greg and Philip, and that evening they went out with the Sonic Ear in the hope of hearing more ghosts, but had they known what they could hear, they would have stayed home. The lads visited the churchyard of Holy Trinity on Fir Lane, and I have had many firsthand experiences of ghostly goings-on in this cemetery, as I once lived close to it in my younger days, and I can vouchsafe that this graveyard has many ghosts, including one of an elderly woman in black with white curly hair, as well as one of a lady in her fifties who died from cancer in the 1950s who seems to be looking for something (some say her own grave) in the cemetery as she roams about in the wee small hours. I – and many others – have also heard a group of children whispering and giggling in the cemetery at all hours in the morning. These are just a few of the ghosts that are active in Holy Trinity churchyard, and this was the venue chosen by the 11-year-old boys that Thursday evening on 24 April 1980. The time was almost 9pm and it began to rain. Philip's mother and sister went in search for him as twilight began to fall across Wavertree, and at one point he hid behind a gravestone with Greg as his mum and sister walked up nearby Fir Lane, shouting his name. The lad thought it was so funny, being so near to the concerned searchers as he hid behind a large black granite headstone with Greg, who was turning red as he bottled in his urge to laugh out loud. Just before 10pm, Greg said it was time he was getting home. There was an eerie stillness in the air, and high above, a gibbous waxing moon shed its feeble silvery light on the graveyard.

The only other illumination was from a single sodium lamp on nearby Fir Lane; for some reason, all of the lamp post lights on Prince Alfred Road – the main road running between the western side of the cemetery and Wavertree Park – were out, and even when lit, Prince Alfred Road (as anyone local will verify) can become rather quiet in the evenings. Philip urged Greg to have one more attempt at eavesdropping on the world of ghosts, but Greg said it was too late, so Philip accused him of being a 'scaredy cat'. Greg said, 'Well you have a go, go 'ead,' and handed him the Sonic Ear. Philip eagerly accepted the invitation and put on the stethoscope earpieces and switched on the toy. He wandered around the moon-silvered cemetery and at first he jumped when he heard a dog barking in the distance somewhere. But then, as he neared Holy Trinity Church – which dated back over two centuries – Philip definitely heard a man's voice, and it sounded like a deep rich voice – almost operatic in timbre, and the lowness of this voice made it sound quite uncanny. 'Greg, did you hear that then?' Philip asked, and Greg shook his head with an annoyed face and reached for the Sonic Ear, but Philip swung it away from his grasp and said, 'No, hang on, I'm hearing voices! Shhh!' At this point, may I point out that both lads were standing on a floor of the cemetery that is paved with the oldest of the gravestones, many of which date back to the 1700s. Both boys were not really aware that they were being disrespectful and many people who use the cemetery routinely walk over these old gravestone flags.

Philip could now hear what almost sounded like monks chanting something, but he couldn't understand just what they were cantillating – perhaps it was something in Latin. But then that eerie voice of unusual lowness intoned a word Philip could understand: 'Arthur McQuale…' – that was the name of Philip's neighbour, a man in his sixties. 'Greg!' Philip's voice went up an octave. He took out one of the ear-pieces and told Greg to listen. At first Greg sulkily said, 'Giz it back,' but Philip swore and urged Greg to listen, and Greg knew from the seriousness of his friend's tone that he had heard something startling. Greg put the ear-piece in his ear and blocked his other ear with the tip of his index finger, and he too could hear that basso voiced stranger reciting names, and most of the names were unknown to the boys, but one of them stood out, because it was the name of Greg's 3-year-old cousin Michelle, who only lived on Newcastle Road, less than a hundred yards away from the cemetery. Greg's stomach turned over and the boy had the growing urge to flee from the place of the dead – but something even more incredible happened, and this incident haunts Greg and Philip to this day. There is a pathway in the cemetery of Holy Trinity which leads from the graveyard gates of Prince Alfred Road, and up this path, there came a single file of faintly glowing green figures, only visible as tiny glow worm pinpoints of light at first, but as the terrified lads looked on, they saw these points join up and form various figures who were walking in their direction. A tall figure in some sort of hooded robe was leading the ghostly procession, and he looked like a monk. Behind him were men, women and children, and they were all walking silently towards the church.

Greg felt the ear-piece being wrenched from his ear as Philip dropped the Sonic Ear and ran like the wind out of the cemetery. The boy leaped up onto the wall on Church Road and was almost hit by a car as he dashed in blind terror across the road. Greg left the Sonic Ear toy on the gravestone flags, where the toy had fallen and broken its listening dish, and he ran as fast as his legs could carry him out of Holy Trinity cemetery.

Both boys were so afraid of what they had seen and heard in that cemetery, neither of them would go back to the graveyard to pick up the broken Sonic Ear, and Greg's grandfather had to go and get it. Both lads had terrible nightmares and Philip in particular was badly affected. He wet the bed regularly after that night in the cemetery and began have terrible runs of bad luck. His next door neighbour Arthur McQuale, died of a heart attack right outside the front door of Philip's house, and then Greg's little 3-year-old cousin Michelle was diagnosed with a rare form of leukaemia and died within weeks.

For over thirty years, Greg and Philip wondered what they had seen and heard in that cemetery, and when Greg met me in 2010, I told him what might have taken place, as far-fetched as my explanation probably sounded. The key to the mystery was the date – the 24 April – St Mark's Eve. Any folklorist and Occultist worth their salt will tell you to take extra care passing cemeteries on that date, because, for some obscure reason which probably dates back to long before the written word, there are certain dates when the Angel of Death (called Angelystor in these parts) will reveal who will die within the parish in the coming year. One date this can occasionally happen is at Halloween – 31 October, and also 30 April - Walpurgis Night (the Devil's Birthday), but St Mark's Eve – April 24, is the most universally recognised date for the foretelling of the dead by the Angel of Death, and that was the very date Greg and Philip went out with an apparently harmless toy listening device to Holy Trinity Churchyard. What the schoolboys had witnessed was a procession of wraiths of the doomed for that year. Across this nation of ours, it was always a ritual of the villagers in olden times to sit in the porch of a church on St Mark's Eve between the hours of 10pm and midnight to see the spectres of those marked for death arrive. They arrived in the order they would die, and with gruesome indications of the manner in which they would die; a rope around a neck, a face pockmarked by some disease, and on one occasion, the wraith of a well-known woman was seen walking nude down the aisle of the church with a dead baby hanging from her left hand by its umbilical cord – and blood was streaming down her legs from what looked like a gaping wound in her vagina. And sure enough, this woman later died of terrible blood loss during childbirth and her babe died too, strangled by its cord. Some occultists say that the wraiths of people having a close shave with death that year would be seen peering into the church but would never cross the threshold. So, you have been warned, on St Mark's Eve, keep well away from churches and their cemeteries.

THE GHOST OF A MURDERER

During World War Two, a particularly brutal murder took place in the Waterloo area of Liverpool. The culprit was eventually brought to justice by an unusual clue which he had left behind at the scene of the crime.

It all began on the stormy evening of 2 November 1940, when fifteen-year-old Mary Hagan left her home in Waterloo to buy cigarettes and a newspaper for her father. When she failed to return from the errand, her father called the police.

The police organised search parties which combed the area and that same night, the body of the missing girl was discovered in a concrete blockhouse, which had been built to serve as an anti-invasion fortress. It was soon evident that the poor girl had been raped as well as murdered. As the detectives searched the ground around the blockhouse for clues, they came upon the distinct impression of a boot heel in the mud. Nearby, more clues were found: a piece of army bandage, stained with a zinc-based ointment that had (from the primitive forensic deductions of that time) been used to treat a thumb wound, and a chocolate bar wrapper which also had small smears of zinc ointment on it. Further forensic analysis revealed that Mary had eaten the chocolate bar. This meant that whoever had worn the bandage had also come into contact with the murdered girl. If the wearer of the bandage could be found, then the police would possibly have their killer.

There were thousands of soldiers stationed in Lancashire at the time, which left the police with the seemingly impossible task of tracing Mary's killer. However, they received a break when a young waitress came forward with a very valuable piece of information. She told detectives how a soldier with a cut on his face had asked her if he could clean himself up in her home. He claimed that he had been involved in a fight.

Then a series of other facts came together which linked the killing with a previous crime. A cyclist named Anne McVittie had been robbed by a soldier on a canal bank just a month earlier, less than a mile from the spot where Mary Hagan had been raped and killed, and the descriptions of the suspect wanted in connection with these crimes were very similar.

A fortnight after the waitress gave her description of the suspicious man, the prime suspect in the murder case, an Irish Guard from Seaforth, Sam Morgan, was arrested in connection with a robbery in London. An observant detective noticed how Private Morgan had a healed scar on his thumb. This information was wired to the Lancashire force, and a search of Morgan's Seaforth home commenced immediately.

A length of army bandage, which exactly matched the strip found at the murder scene, was retrieved from Morgan's house. Then more witnesses came forward to underline the soldier's guilt. The landlord of a public house told police how he had seen Morgan in his pub on the night of the murder, sporting a bloodstained cap. Furthermore, Morgan's boots perfectly matched the plaster cast that had been made from the footprint found next to the body.

Now certain that they had got their man, the detectives arrested Morgan and led him away for questioning. He betrayed his guilt by his feeble smile and twitching facial muscles, as he lamely tried to insist that he had only robbed cigarettes and money from Mary, and had not brutally assaulted and killed her. The evidence against Morgan was overwhelming and at his trial he was found guilty of the rape and murder of Mary Hagan. He was subsequently hanged on 4 April 1941, at Kirkdale Gaol. That summer, it is said that at the home of Sam Morgan, the ghostly outline of the murderer appeared whenever any of his relatives mentioned him, and he would cry out, 'Let me rest in peace!' as he paced up and down, and sometimes the tormented spectre would cry out in agony and objects would be smashed against the walls. On one occasion, the poker in the unlit fire began to rock in the grate – then attacked a couple of people who were reminiscing about Mary Hagan. In the end, a priest performed the Rites of Exorcism at the house, and during the ritual, a terrifying apparition of Sam Morgan was seen in the corner of the parlour, surrounded by flames which crept up his body as he screamed. Deep unholy laughter echoed throughout the house and the words recited by the priest were heard to echo and somehow reverse as he spoke them. The exorcism ended with a massive fall of soot from the chimney which sent black clouds billowing throughout the parlour. After that, the tortured ghost of the killer was seen no more.

IN THE TWINKLING OF AN EYE

In the year 1815 at a harsh Prussian prison in Weichselmunde, a prisoner named Diderici – a former valet of who had been jailed for impersonating his master after the latter had died from a stroke – was walking in the prison yard (which was enclosed by extra-thick walls 20 feet in height), chained and manacled to a line of other prisoners during the short time the inmates were allowed to exercise in the outdoors. One of the prisoners noticed something strange happening to the body of the disgraced valet as he walked ahead of him – it was becoming transparent. The startled prisoner drew the attentions of the other prisoners to this remarkable phenomenon, and then the guards of the Prussian prison also saw what was happening and looked on with a mixture of awe and fear. Diderici faded away into nothingness and the manacles and shackles he had worn fell with a loud clank to the ground – and the prisoner never reappeared again and his fate remains a mystery. The superstitious believed the Devil had come to collect the former valet's soul, and in such unenlightened times, this mystery was classed as one of those insoluble conundrums that are reported from time to time that are usually associated with evil spirits and Lucifer, but nearer to home, here on Merseyside, there have been similar unexplained vanishing acts in modern times. One case of apparent teleportation comes to mind, and this was reported to me several years ago.

In 1961, a 40-year-old compulsive gambler named Harry Hammonde borrowed £300 from a notorious loan-shark in Huyton, and the deal was to pay back £750 in five monthly instalments of £150 – but, of course, as soon as Harry got his £300 he bought a Ford Anglia, took his girlfriend down to Bournemouth then returned home and within days he blew what was left of his loan on restaurants, cigars, whisky, brown ale and the horses. Harry was coming out of a Bernard Murphy betting shop in Everton one afternoon when a towering amateur boxer seized him by the lapels of his coat and reminded him he had three days to cough up the first repayment instalment to his boss. Harry tremblingly assured the lackey he'd have the money on time and the boxer pressed his colossal fist hard against Harry's jaw, then walked off. Three days came and went, and Harry had plans to relocate to Birkenhead, but his Ford Anglia had to be put in a garage on the dock road after developing engine trouble, and after Harry left the garage, he walked right into that boxer again. 'Where's the money?' the pugilist enquired and out came the excuses which cut no ice, and so the boxer looked around; no witnesses. He drew back his fist, ready to strike. His other huge hand gripped Harry's coat lapels. 'No!' Harry cried, closed his eyes – and suddenly he had a sensation of falling, as if he was in a lift in free-fall after the cable had snapped. Then came the sound of an ear-splitting vehicle horn. Harry opened his eyes. A Leyland eight-wheel lorry thundered past, missing him by inches. Harry found himself on Conway Street – Birkenhead – in the middle of a busy road. Harry wandered off and finally realised he had somehow travelled one-and-a-half miles in a split second. Harry telephoned his girlfriend and arranged for her to meet him in Hamilton Square, and the couple later moved to Chester to settle down to a new life. This teleportation case remains a tantalizing mystery. Harry Hammonde passed away in the 1970s but his daughter Elaine told me how, over the years, he often mentioned the bizarre teleportation incident, and how he believed God or some guardian angel was responsible for saving his neck at the hands of the boxer that day. The shock of travelling across the River Mersey in the twinkling of an eye convinced Harry that some kind of divine intervention had saved him for a reason, and so he turned over a new leaf and never set foot inside a betting shop again.

One afternoon in 2011 I was about to leave the studios of a radio station in Liverpool after talking on air about an assortment of local hauntings and mysteries, when the station receptionist told me a man wanted to see me, and she nodded to a silver-haired man of about seventy who was sitting in the 'Performance Space' where several other members of the public sit sipping coffee, tea or soft drinks as they watch the radio presenters on air through a window of soundproof glass. This man who had asked to see me was now retired, but in his younger days he had spent about fifteen years in the police force, and he had a strange tale to tell me. His name was Hugh. One foggy evening in 1970, at around 11pm, Hugh and another policeman named Stan were in their patrol car (a Mini Cooper), which had just set out from the police station on Derby Lane (which was located between Old Swan and Stoneycroft), when the fog in front of their vehicle became so thick, the policemen couldn't even see the light from the lamp posts ahead. Stan, who was driving the car, wisely slowed down, and remarked about the opaqueness of the fog. About thirty seconds passed, when suddenly the fog thinned quite suddenly, and Stan and Hugh found themselves staring in disbelief at the scene beyond the windscreen – it was Orwell Avenue, just a stone's throw from Westminster Road Police Station. Somehow, within half a minute, in a police car travelling in a northerly direction at a speed of less than 20 miles per hour, the two officers had travelled almost four thousand yards in a north westerly direction to another district of Liverpool and into another police division. Stan halted the patrol car, turned to his colleague and seemed speechless for a moment. He swore, which was not at all like Stan, and then he looked at the church on Orwell Avenue (which has since been renamed Orwell Road), and he asked Hugh: 'Do you remember us getting here? I don't.'

'What the heck – ' Hugh said, and the two policemen sat in the motionless car, both completely lost for an explanation. Hugh suggested reporting the strange incident to Chief Superintendent Jones – if he was on duty at Westminster Road police station, but Stan said they'd be hauled before a psychiatrist if they mentioned what had just happened. Instead, Stan drove back to the Old Swan Division and the patrol continued as normal, although both officers often talked about the weird incident for months. Then, around 1971, Hugh was once again with Stan in a patrol car on London Road at half-past one on a wintry morning. The officers had investigated a call from the member of the public who had said he thought a jeweller's shop was being broken into on London Road, but the caller had either been mistaken or it had been a hoax call, for the shop was secured and there were no signs of anyone suspicious about upon this morning. As the police patrol car reached Pembroke Place on its way back to Old Swan, the windscreen seemed to freeze over, and everything became fuzzy to the officers as they looked at the road ahead. Then, just as quickly as the 'ice' had formed on the windscreen, it rapidly evaporated, and now the policemen found themselves on a street neither of them knew. The street seemed suburban, and there was a bowling green to the left of the car – which, it transpired, now had its bonnet pointed to the west (opposite the direction it had been heading). 'I Don't believe it,' Hugh said, and gingerly opened the door of the vehicle and stepped out onto the black-iced road. The street-name plaque said the cops were now in Marshfield Road, Norris Green. In the proverbial twinkling of an eye the two policemen and their patrol car had somehow been transported nearly five thousand yards – well over two miles. Once again Hugh and Stan deemed it wise to say nothing to their superiors or colleagues, but the policemen were naturally fascinated and intrigued by these acts of teleportation, and while Stan eventually forgot about the experiences, Hugh began to take an interest in the paranormal and read all he could on the subject. He also heard about colleagues who had found themselves experiencing lost chunks of time in certain parts of the city which could never be explained, and Hugh catalogued all of these incidents with a view to one day publishing them in the form of a book. Instead, Hugh handed the collected material to me. Hugh believes that Stan, who sadly passed away a few years ago, had something to do with the teleportings, and he might be right, as I believe that some cases of teleportation are triggered by some psychic energy, and perhaps Stan unknowingly activated the power behind them. I mentioned the teleportation incidents experienced by Hugh and Stan on the radio (having first sought mission from Hugh to do so) and a very strange development took place; a former convicted criminal named Jimmy who had been in the vicinity of Pembroke Place on the night the patrol car was supernaturally transferred to Norris Green, contacted me after listening to my broadcast and said that he and a friend he didn't want to name had seen the patrol car vanish before their eyes that morning around 1.40 am. 'One second it was there, moving along, and then it was just gone,' Jimmy told me. He had then continued trying – unsuccessfully – to break into a pub. I asked Jimmy to meet Hugh and the policeman confirmed that Jimmy was telling the truth because he had described the very car and even the exact position of the vehicle when it had vanished. Just what causes these teleportations, be it individuals, vehicles, animate or inanimate objects, remains a mystery for the moment. As you read this, research is going on in labs across the world into teleportation, which has been actually achieved with photons and other sub-atomic particles using laser beams. It's only a matter before some genius makes a breakthrough which could see atoms and molecules being beamed from one place to the next, and this will result in technology which will make most forms of transportation obsolete; it will be bad news for the aviation and car industry when teleportation will allow you to visit any holiday destination on this earth – and off it – at the speed of light. It *will* happen one day.

HENRY

Apple-sweet scents drifted on zephyrs from Stanley Park that summer and found their way to the button nose of 7-year-old Silvia as she leaned on the windowsill, gazing up into the baby blue sky. The window of the back bedroom in Auntie Peg's had been lifted open, and the sun of July 1968 was pouring in, along with the hubbub of distant traffic noise of Walton Road and the faint voices of Pugin Street. A ginger cat was stretched out in the sun atop of a backyard wall where ferns sprouted and greenbottle and bluebottle flies blundered into them - and in the west, a morning moon was sinking sleepily behind a chimney pot, soon to be lost in the summer haze. Old Mr Hayes was sitting in his backyard in a deckchair next door doing a crossword as his transistor radio played Cliff Richard singing *Congratulations*. Silvia was just going to shout to him when Auntie Peg came in the room.

'Silvia! Close that window! You'll have the bees and wasps coming in!' she came and dragged the window down and rearranged the net curtains, and Silvia went downstairs, where her favourite Auntie, Mo, was sitting in the parlour. She was younger than Peggy and always said yes instead of no. Silvia was hugging her when she suddenly smelt something. 'I can smell a baby,' the girl announced, and Mo shot a perplexed but bemused look at her niece and her pulsating nostrils.

'Don't talk daft, Silvia, now go out and play,' said Peggy, coming into the parlour.

'No, honest, babies have this smell,' Silvia explained to her aunties, and she described the scent as a sort of cross between the odours of certain perfumed talcs, a Milky Bar and Persil soap powder, and more worryingly, Silvia asserted that whenever she detected "baby smell" one always appeared not long after.

Auntie Mo was no longer smiling and seemed tearful. Silvia didn't know Mo was barren, but later as she eavesdropped on the aunts from the hallway, she discovered that Mo and her husband had tried for a baby for ten years. That very week though, Mo became ill – and this sickness came upon her every time she woke up. She went to the doctor and tests were carried out. Auntie Mo was having bouts of morning sickness, because she was pregnant – but how did Silvia know this? Auntie Peggy said it had been a coincidence, because no one could tell if a woman was going to have a baby because of some mysterious smell – it was ridiculous.

Silvia stayed at her Auntie Peg's a month later, and something even stranger took place: a 'shadow baby' as Silvia called it, began to visit the girl. And at first Silvia was a little scared, but soon looked at the entity as a friend. It never spoke, moved in a sort of jerky way, and seemed two-dimensional, like someone had cut the shape of a baby out of a piece of black card. It reminded Silvia of Henry, the baby featured on the bottles of Fairy washing-up liquid. This entity made its debut on top of the old wardrobe in the spare room Sylvia was staying in, and Silvia went to tell her aunt, but she couldn't see the baby and thought it was just the product of a childish imagination.

One moonlit night at Auntie Peg's, Silvia was awakened by something tickling her nose as she slept in her bed. It was him, the silhouetted baby boy, and on this occasion, he seemed to make a faint chuckling sound as he touched the girl's nose. The baby smell was back and almost stifling, and Silvia now realised that he was the source of that baby scent. He danced and spun like a top on the chequered quilt in the moonlight and Silvia laughed so loud, Auntie Peg rapped on the wall. 'Who are you?' she asked the living shadow, and he never uttered a word in reply. He jumped on the rail at the end of the bed and walked along it with his arms stretched out like a tight-rope artist. Then he played hide and seek with Silvia by melting into natural shadows in the moonlight and springing out on her when she'd get frustrated because she couldn't find him.

That week Silvia visited her Uncle Freddie and

Auntie Jean in New Brighton, and there was a young woman there named Cynthia, who worked for Freddie, and she had the baby smell, according to Silvia. Freddie told Silvia to be quiet, and shouted at her, which was not like Freddie at all, for he was usually a happy-go-lucky man who would always take Silvia to the fairground or Southport beach, but years later, Silvia learned that Cynthia had been having Freddie's baby, but his wife hadn't known that when Silvia visited that day.

Silvia kept wanting to stay with Auntie Peggy, just to see the Shadow Baby, and she would cry and throw terrible tantrums when her mother said she couldn't stay over. Silvia's mum began to worry when her daughter would speak incessantly about "Henry" and his antics, but the girl's father said it was just just a case of Silvia's innocent imagination running rampant, and that she'd soon grow out of it. On one occasion, an audacious would-be burglar tried to get into Aunt Peggy's house through the open window where Silvia was lying awake one evening while it was still light, and the shade of the little ghostly baby jumped up onto the ledge, scaring him so much, he fell backwards off his ladder and must have sustained some terrible injuries when he landed on the backyard wall on his back. The criminal crawled off the wall, falling into the entry to crawl away as Silvia raised the alarm. The Shadow Baby had saved the day, but, of course, Peggy didn't believe that, and she warned Silvia to stop leaving her bedroom window open – night *or* day.

Sadly, a year later, Peggy suddenly died from what seems to have been a severe asthma attack. On the day of Peg's funeral, Silvia paid her last visit to the house on Pugin Street, and before she left for good she saw "Henry" waving from the top of the stairs. She ran up the stairs in tears to go to him, but he vanished. Not long after that, Silvia's ability to smell the lovely scent of the unborn was lost. Why had that ghostly babe haunted that house in Pugin Street? When she was old enough, Silvia's mum told her that long ago, Peggy had given birth to a stillborn child in that room where Silvia had slept during her sleepovers, and at the time of the tragic birth, Peggy had been unmarried. The father had been a well-known man who was looked upon as a pillar of the community, and had the news of the pregnancy leaked out it would have ruined his career and probably ended his marriage. Could this hidden incident have been the reason for the Shadow Baby? Across the world, there are increasing reports of what are known as shadow people, which, as the name suggests, refers to silhouetted figures of people that are seen by people from all walks of life. Some think the shadow people are just a type of evil ghost, but other researchers into the paranormal have hypothesised that they are visitants from a parallel world or some other dimension. "Henry" could have been one of these beings, although in light of the sad history of the spare room on Pugin Street, perhaps this isn't the case.

TRUTH BE TOLD

There have been controversial reports in the media in recent times of computerised "lie detectors" – voice-stress analysers to give them their proper title – being used in certain parts of the country to evaluate the validity of Council Tax claimants as they talk to benefit advisors on the telephone. This totalitarian technology has not been used to analyse the verbal statements of MPs for obvious reasons, and therein lies a Catch 22 situation; the State eagerly uses the latest technology to identify liars, but those in power will never be the subject of such scrutiny themselves, because lies are the cornerstone of all politics, and as Juvenal once remarked, "Quis custodiet ipsos custodes?" which can be rendered as "Who watches the watchers?" In other words, who keeps and eye on the people who keep an eye on us?

With an infallible lie detector we'd know, for example, whether the Archbishop of Canterbury actually believed in God and a lot of other truths would come to light. In the world of the Occult, there have been many documented claims about the devising of "truth spells" and the creation of all sorts of magical devices that can act as a lie detector, and one of the most grisly pieces of arcane apparatus to single out liars is the Bocca della Verità – the Mouth of Truth. This is the graven image of a certain demon's face in marble (but it can also be cast in clay) with a wide slot-like mouth which the person to be tested places his or her hand in. If the person lies, a finely-balanced blade mechanism slices off the fingers. An elderly occultist and supreme astrologer named Richard Parkinson constructed one of these contrivances in the cellar of 26 Horatio Street, off Scotland Road, in the summer of 1852. Parkinson had acquired the plans to create the Mouth of Truth from a copy of a manuscript drawn up by Britain's greatest astrologer, Dr John Dee, occult adviser to Elizabeth I and a secret agent (whose code number was, believe it or not, 007, and I wonder if this was known to James Bond creator Ian Fleming).

Richard Parkinson carried out his thriving astrology business over his son's joinery shop by day, and although the practice was technically illegal, Parkinson was not bothered by the police. He charged customers sixpence to have their fortune told, and he would look into a crystal ball and somehow come up with eerily accurate readings. People from all walks of life, from doctors to dockers, had to book appointments to see the Scotland Road Seer, as he widely known, and Parkinson had a bulging bank account because of his thriving business. The popular astrologer used some of the capital raised by his business to construct a Mouth of Truth in his cellar, and this was completed in June 1852. Parkinson's son, John, warned his father about creating the dangerous lie detector, for who would be foolish enough to even attempt to test it? 'The police would,' was the father's reply, and he told John he wished to lease out the device to the law courts, and actually invited prominent police inspector named Jack Amos to see the device. Amos amusingly put his hand in the mouth of the wall-mounted marble disk and sneered at its weird face, which was encircled by inscribed signs of the Zodiac. Now it was time to test the strange medallion-shaped device.

'Have you ever murdered a woman?' Parkinson asked, and the inspector said, 'No,' and then he cried out in agony and withdrew his hand, but the tips of his middle and index fingers were missing! The inspector almost fainted, and red rivulets of fresh blood trickled from the mouth of the graven face. With blood squirting from the stumps of his fingers, Amos cursed the astrologer and promised him he'd have him jailed for his satanic work, and he climbed the stairs groaning, leaving a trail of blood behind him, then left the shop, where he urged a member of the public to hail a carriage that would take him to the infirmary. Jack Amos was just one of the many detectives later arrested after a large-scale investigation into corruption within the Liverpool Police. Parkinson was arrested, charged with obtaining money by deception, and imprisoned for three months. Inspector Jack Amos instructed two officers to destroy the graven idol known as the Mouth of Truth with sledgehammers, and this was duly done. Officers also ransacked the attic of 26 Horatio Street, removed all the books on astrology and the occult, and burned them in a heap in the backyard. When Richard Parkinson had served his three months, he was arrested again when he tried to set up his fortune-telling business in another part of the city, and in the end he had to move to Chester to carry on his trade, but its unknown whether he tried to recreate the Bocca della Verità. Truth, according to the old proverbs, can walk through the world unarmed, and it will always prevail, and although lies travel swiftly, the truth always overtakes them, but ask yourself this question: if someone invented a foolproof lie-detector, would you let someone test it out on *you*?

UNREQUITED

In the mid-Eighties, a selfish, suspicious, sarcastic and deceitful Garston man in his mid-thirties named Ian began to receive what we could term as "love letters" from an admirer who signed her name as Fleur. Ian, who held a job as a Council clerk in the Municipal Buildings on Dale Street, initially thought the letters were the work of one of his workmates, but when he showed the letters to his mother, Irene, she said they not only seemed genuine, the handwriting also looked distinctly feminine and whoever this Fleur was, according to Irene, she was very romantic. 'Maybe it'd do you good to go out with a girl like her after all the trollops you've had,' Irene told her son, but he callously crumpled the letter up and hurled it in the kitchen bin. 'She sounds dead old in those letters,' Ian reasoned, recalling the quaint turns of phrase in the missives, and he put on his Slazenger jumper straight from the tumble dryer and said, 'If I want a granny I'll go to the Grafton.'

On the following morning as he ate breakfast, he asked his mother to turn the radio down as Terry Wogan was making his hangover worse. Manilla envelopes, and a pale blue tell-tale one, plopped through the letter-box, and Ian's mum smiled and said, 'Ooh, looks like Fleur's written to you again.' She picked up the love letter and the bills and Ian said, 'Throw it in the bin, she's a divvy,' but his mother opened it and read it. She was almost in tears by the time she finished the letter from Fleur. 'Aw, lad, she says here, "as I write this letter, there's just me and the cat up at this hour, and the chances are, you're fast asleep. I've never felt so alone. We'll probably never meet. So many people have soulmates in this world, and the tragedy is that they never get to meet them." Aw, isn't that sad?'

Ian put his index finger in his mouth and pretended to be sick. A week later another letter arrived, only this time it bore a Wirral postmark (whereas the previous letters had been posted in the Liverpool 19 area, according to the franking mark on the envelope) . Ian's mother read it and said, 'She said she's ill, and probably won't have the strength to write again for a good while.'

'Good,' Ian retorted, and watched the telly.

'I'm dead intrigued over these letters,' Irene confessed, squinting at the lovely calligraphy on the Basildon Bond stationery. 'Are you sure you don't know anyone called Fleur?'

'No,' was Ian's monosyllabic reply.

Three days after this, Ian got dressed up for a Saturday night out. First he went to the Everyman Bistro, then it was the wine lodge, and then onto his usual pub crawl around Hope, Hardman and Leece Streets. On this night he left Ye Cracke on Rice Street, and made his way over to Kirklands wine bar, and as he crossed Hardman Street, a female voice behind him called his name. He turned and saw a woman, probably in her late sixties, with a head of permed curly hair, and she wore a pair of thick "pebble-lensed" glasses. Ian returned a blank look, and the stranger grinned and said, 'It's me - Fleur. I've just been to the Philharmonic,' she said, and the admission stunned Ian. This woman had to be unbalanced, he thought.

So this was the romantic old biddy that'd had a crush on him. 'Have you been following me?' Ian asked, and looked her up and down, taking in all of the outdated attire.

'No, I just noticed you – ' Fleur said, and had tears in her eyes. 'I died today you see, and well, it doesn't matter, goodbye Ian.'

She vanished before his eyes. Ian felt numb with shock. He sat drinking all night in Kirklands, and it seemed as if every girl in the place was on his case, and yet he could hardly speak to any of them, because he kept thinking of the way that woman had vanished before his very eyes. She had looked solid. She had looked as alive as anyone else as she spoke to him. When Ian got home he told his mother what had happened, and she knew her son was an unimaginative bore, not prone to invent stories of this sort, and so she made the sign of the cross, and she looked as if she was about to burst into tears.

'I'm terrified I'll see her again now,' Ian admitted, and that night he slept with his bedroom light on.

Another letter arrived from Fleur in the morning. It had been written the day before she had died, and in the letter, Fleur said she was in Clatterbridge Hospital, dying from cancer. She didn't have long, and wished she could go to a concert at the Philharmonic with Ian, as she loved classical music. She wrote: "We'll probably never meet; unrequited love is the only love that lasts forever. I'm sorry if I pestered you with my letters. You reminded me of a man I loved – and lost – a long, long time ago. I suppose I should know better at my age, but inside I'm still the same girl I was when I was sixteen. Goodbye Ian."

A STRANGE FORCE OF ATTRACTION

The March wind from the Mersey was as sharp as a whetted knife that afternoon in 2011, when two women in their fifties hurried through Liverpool One shopping complex, intending to go to the Apple store, but instead, another glacial wind which came from the north, swept down Paradise Street and pummelled the women - Enid and Liz – towards the John Lewis store. Enid was the smaller and more petite of the two, and she was particularly susceptible to the freak icy gale, and as she stumbled backwards through the automatic sliding doors of the store, she really appreciated the warmth of the air-conditioning, but cursed the bizarre weather. She patted her head of permed curls with her gloved hand and then took out a tissue from her coat pocket to dab the tears from her stinging eyes. Liz gasped for breath as she careered into the store after Enid.

'You okay Liz?' Enid asked her friend, thinking the gale force blast had given her an asthma attack.

'*What* is going on with this weather?' Liz said between gulps of air, 'I have never seen anything like that. It could have blown us through the plate glass windows.'

'Biggest mistake they made was building Liverpool One so near to the river,' Enid griped, 'talk about the windy city.'

'Let's go and have a coffee upstairs till that dies down,' Liz suggested, looking at a huge canvas banner that had been strung between buildings for some promotion being blown down Paradise Street as shoppers ran out of its path.

The women walked through the menswear towards the escalator.

'We'll have a nice coffee and a scone with some jam and clotted cream, eh?' Liz suggested to Enid, and the both of them laughed.

'An ill wind blows somebody good,' Enid remarked with a chuckle, and she and Liz stepped onto the escalator and rode it up to the first floor. On the way up, Enid squinted at a sign below on the bottom floor and asked Liz: 'Can you see what that says? That sign in blue with the white writing?'

'Yeah,' Liz replied, 'Tommy Hillfiger, why?'

'It was just a blur to me,' Enid told her, and squinted, but the sign was soon lost to sight as they reached the first floor. 'Must get my eyes checked.'

They went to the toilets, readjusted their hair, reapplied lipstick, and then went to the café. As they waited in the queue, the women looked through the large windows, and they could see that the sun had now broken through the grey sky and the winds had apparently died down. Enid ordered a carrot cake and a cup of Earl Grey, and Liz was served a coffee and a mouth-watering scone, strawberry jam and clotted cream. The friends parked themselves at a table in the centre of the café and laughed at the way the wind from out of nowhere had literally forced them into John Lewis. And then in the course of her usually nosy survey of the room, Liz noticed a woman in her sixties at a nearby table, and she was holding the hand of a man half her age. Out the side of her mouth, Liz whispered to Enid: 'Don't look yet, but there's a woman, and she looks about sixty-five, and she's holding the hands of this young fellah who looks as if he could be her son.'

Enid went to turn around, but Liz told her not to just yet – or it would be plainly obvious that she was jangling about the woman in question.

Enid slowly turned, pretending to look out the window, and she said, 'Oh yes, the way the weather's changed for the better now,' but then she looked at the table indicated by Liz's eyes, and saw the woman for herself, apparently 'carrying on' with the young man.

'Talk about a hint of a tint, eh?' Liz murmured, referring to the woman's hair, which looked jet black.

Enid grinned, and began to eat the carrot cake.

Through closed teeth, Liz somehow whispered, 'He's kissing her hand.'

Enid turned and looked straight at the couple.

The young man was standing, and the woman with the dyed head of hair had her hand lifted to his face, and he was kissing her knuckle. 'Thank you, ' he said, 'I will definitely be in touch with you again. Bye.'

And he walked away, and turned back once to wave to the woman.

'Maybe there's hope for us yet,' Enid whispered to Liz and sipped her tea.

'Ha! I can't be bothered with all that rubbish anymore,' Liz said a dismissive wave of her hand, and she began to peel back the little golden lid of the tiny plastic packet of butter.

'Don't you miss having a man about the place?' Enid said with a lopsided smirk, for she knew this subject always kicked her friend off.

'Too old for all that carrying on nowadays. I'd rather sit in bed with a good book or watch a decent film. All that slobbering, kisses and slush. It's all my arse. When I was young I really believed in romance and true love, and er – what's the other one they drum into us? Soulmates. Well we end up more like sole mates, trod on and used as a doormat.'

'So I'll take that as a no,' joked Enid, who had lost her husband seven years ago to cancer, but now and then talked of him in the present tense. She'd say things like, 'Brian says that' or 'Brian does that,' as if he was still around.

'Before I lived with Tom, we were the best of friends, as you well know,' Liz reminisced, with a bitter sweet look in her eyes, 'but they say that once love puts its oar in, friendship is out for good.'

With a piece of cake poised before her mouth, Enid earnestly asked: 'Don't you miss him though, Liz? He was funny. He was witty. I always remember the time he said – '

'Oh let's not talk about him, Enid,' Liz curtailed the trip down memory lane, 'he's not worth talking about. That's a chapter of my life I want to forget.'

Enid ate the carrot cake, then shot a strange look at Liz, who thought her friend was either choking on the cake or having a funny turn, or a 'tropical' as she called her hot flushes.

'You okay?' Liz queried, even more concerned now, because Enid's face was going pink.

Enid nodded.

'What's up? Has that stuck in your throat?' Liz asked, and leaned over towards her friend with an anxious look.

'No,' said Enid at last, in a very low voice. There was an annoying pause from her, then she leaned forward, grasped Liz's fist, and whispered. 'He's in here.'

'What? Who is?'

'Tom, he's sitting behind you,' Enid told her friend, staring over her shoulder.

Liz thought Enid was joking at first, because they had just been talking about Tom, but then she could see that Enid was deadly serious. Liz became lost for words, and seemed to freeze for a moment, and then her plucked eyebrows dipped and furrows formed between them. 'Are you sure?' she asked, mouthing the words almost inaudibly.

Enid nodded. 'Yeah – have a look.'

Liz turned slowly around and saw it was indeed Tom. He was sitting with his back to her, reading a copy of the *Liverpool Echo*.

'Talk of the Devil, eh?' Enid said, and let go of

her friend's hand.

Liz looked to her left, and the woman who had been holding the hand of the young man earlier on was gazing straight at her. Her eyes were very dark and Liz thought there was something foreign about the woman's complexion. The way she was staring at Liz made her feel very uneasy, and to Enid, she said, 'Who's she gawping at?'

'Who?' Enid asked over the rim of her teacup.

'The 'arl one who was with the toyboy,' Liz told her.

The woman in question suddenly rose from her table and came over to Liz, who wondered if the stranger had overheard her talking about her unnaturally black hair and her young man.

'Excuse me, but may I tell you something?' the woman asked Liz. Her accent betrayed her east European origins.

Liz didn't know what to say, but braced herself for a possible insult.

'I'm a Romany fortune teller, and I read palms and all that. I really do,' the woman said, matter of fact.

'It's alright love, I don't have a future to read , and I'm skint anyway,' Liz told her and sipped her coffee. Enid turned to look up at the woman and now it made some sense. She had been holding that young man's hand – had she been reading his palm?

'No, I don't want to tell you your future, I just wanted to say that you have a wonderful aura about you. Very beautiful colours,' the Romany lady informed her with a smile, and looked above and around Liz as if she was studying something invisible to normal eyes.

'Oh, that's nice to know,' Liz replied with so much sarcasm in her voice.

The Romany woman then added: 'And that man behind you has the very same aura, and he must be related to you because his aura is touching yours and they are like - mingling - is that the word?'

And the Romany woman was glancing at Tom, who now turned to see who was talking about auras. He recognised Enid first, smiled, and said, 'Oh, hiya,' but then his smile evaporated instantly when he realised Liz was sitting opposite Enid with her back to him, and to this back, Tom said 'Hiya Liz,' in a rather flat voice.

'Do you know one another?' the alleged fortune teller asked, and Liz nodded.

The exotic-looking woman then smiled and said, 'I thought so,' and returned to her table, where she took her coat from the back of her chair, put it on, then grabbed her bag and walked away. Liz wanted to go after the gypsy, but was too proud to do so. She wanted to know more about the 'shared auras'. Was there some metaphysical bond with Tom, because it always seemed that, no matter how many times she had fallen out with him over the years, they always seemed to be brought together by the strangest forces of circumstance. Then Liz recalled the powerful wind from nowhere which had practically driven her and Enid into the John Lewis store. Liz had been intending to go to the Apple shop to buy an Apple Mac for her brother's birthday, but that bizarre gale had other plans for her.

'Are yous having a drink?' came a familiar voice from behind.

'No, it's alright Tom,' Enid said with a bright smile, 'How have you been diddling?'

And eventually, Liz and Enid went to Tom's table, and they talked. Tom could hardly keep eye contact at first, but then over many cups of tea, and coffee he became more relaxed, as did Liz, and in the midst of the conversation, Tom said a strange thing. He had been ready to leave the café at one point earlier on that afternoon, before Liz and Enid had arrived, but he had developed this strange overriding hunch to stay put, and he had the mounting feeling that if he did stay where he was, his luck would change for the better. Then Liz recalled another strange thing. Nearly twenty years ago, just after the first split from Tom, she had a ridiculous urge to go to Rhyl, and she went, even though it was pouring with rain, and at the Welsh resort she met Tom at the fairground. It was as if something – some Cosmic Romantic up there was acting as Cupid with all of these strategic coincidences. Liz mentioned these incidences of synchronicity, and Tom recalled even more of them. 'Maybe that Romany woman was genuine after all, eh Liz?' Enid mused, thinking of the remarks about the shared aura. The three friends left the café and walked out onto a sunny Paradise Street.

THE DELHI EYE

In the 1970s a certain Liverpool shopkeeper painted the word "SEX" in signal-red on a white board measuring some six feet by four feet, and he placed this audacious eye-catching sign in his store window in a desperate effort to drum up business – and it worked. Even the adverse publicity generated by the controversial sign got the shop noticed, but if you look around you today in Liverpool, you will be greeted by mostly mediocre window displays. The Victorians were much better at self-promotion when it came to plugging their trade. On one occasion a Victorian tea-room owner on Church Street hired a giraffe from a zoo and tethered it outside his premises to attract hundreds of customers, and in 1893, at 54 Church Street, where Primark now stands, a curious object appeared in the window of James B.G. Peters the Jeweller – a massive 16-inch-diameter crystal ball. The banner above it in the window promised: "See Your Future

HERE in a Crystal Ball! Genuine Crystal Ball from Delhi". The crystal ball in question had been purchased from a Sergeant Major Christopher Jordan, a rough diamond of a man who had served in India for forty-five years. Jordan had "acquired" the 'Delhi Eye' – a sphere of pure quartz, from a fakir, but claimed it was unlucky, and so he sold it to Mr Peters the jeweller for thirty guineas. Upon the first day the oversized crystal ball was installed in the window of the jeweller's store, the unusual gimmick attracted a large crowd as the curious gazed at the beguiling sphere, mounted on a shelf of green velvet among the arrays of rings, brooches, watches and other precious adornments. But as darkness gathered late that afternoon, a rumour swept Church Street and beyond: strange faces and various ghostly figures were being seen in the "Delhi Eye" – and Mr James the jeweller also saw these. Mr James distinctly saw a man in a turban looking at him with an angry penetrating stare; was this the fakir who had once owned the huge scrying globe, perhaps? Some people who gazed into the Delhi Eye claimed to see the fierce face of a tiger, and one wonders if this was a Bengal tiger, given the crystal ball's country of origin. A respected rival jeweller, William Harold Gordon, accused Mr Peters of conning the public through the use of a hidden "magic lantern", but Peters swore there was no trickery, and allowed Mr Gordon to examine the crystal ball. Surrounded by a crushing crowd inside the shop, Mr Gordon inspected the weighty fifty-pound globe, and recoiled in horror, for he saw a woman's face appear in the Delhi Eye – and it was his wife's face, and she was with a well-known gentleman – a Mr Harrison, a friend of Gordon's family. Mr Gordon seemed unsteady as he saw his wife Margaret kissing Harrison, and he could see now – as everyone else could – that the adulterers were naked! Mr Gordon lifted his cane and brought it down on the Delhi Eye, intending to shatter it, but his cane broke in two. Mr Peters and two employees set on the enraged Mr Gordon and wrestled with him, and in the ensuing mêlée, some of the onlookers in the store stole rings and watches. Police whistles were soon shrieking in unholy harmony on Church Street, and Mr Gordon tried, unsuccessfully, to have Peters arrested for his "scurrilous deception", but when detectives and police looked in the Delhi Eye they could see nothing supernatural at all. Mrs Gordon later admitted to her affair with Mr Harrison, and Mr Gordon brought proceedings against his wife and the latter in the divorce court, and Harrison had to pay £500 damages. Mr Gordon had wed his wife at St Luke's Church on 2 October 1883, and had enjoyed a married life for ten years, but in recent months Mrs Gordon had become infatuated with Harrison, and their affair was one of the best-kept secrets in Liverpool - so how on earth had Mr James the jeweller found out about the infidelity and shamelessly used his knowledge to ruin Mr Harold by some jiggery pokery with a so-called crystal ball? People swore Mr James had nothing to do with any legerdemain. The crystal ball was left in the window for three days, and people swore they could see uncanny sights in it. A woman who became mesmerised by the Delhi Eye fainted when she saw her husband hanging himself, but its not known if this ever came to pass, or whether the woman imagined the macabre scene.

The Crystal ball proved to be too popular, and on several occasions attempts were made to steal it, and Peters felt as if the quartz globe was harming his reputation as a respected jeweller, so he sold it for an undisclosed sum to a Wavertree Road jeweller named James Farebrother, and he claimed the ghost of a tiger had subsequently attacked him on his premises a day after receiving the Delhi Eye. The crystal ball was stolen from Farebrother's shop, along with 12 silver chains and 72 rings in June 1897. The robbers – 28-year-old John Mason and his accomplice, 37-year-old Ada Simon, were caught after the latter tried to pledge one of the stolen items at a pawn shop on St Anne Street. The pawn broker recognised the purloined item as belonging to one of the stolen pieces supplied to him by the Liverpool Police, and he quickly sent for a constable. The robbers, it transpired, had co-habited at a house on Claypole Street, off Earle Road in Edge Hill, but when detectives searched the thieves' hideout, the Delhi Eye was nowhere to be found, and it turned out that a friend of John Mason had stolen the crystal ball and sold it to someone in a public house for thirty shillings. The Delhi Eye was never recovered and its whereabouts are still unknown.

A NIGHT WITH A DEAD MAN

The following story is said to have taken place in a certain well-known church in northern Liverpool in the late 19th century. At a gentleman's club on Bold Street, a wealthy wine-dealer named Charles was said to be a vicious sceptic of anything relating to what we would nowadays terms as the paranormal. In Victorian times, the term was, of course, the supernatural, and anything pertaining to this sphere, be it ghosts, table turning, séances, the reading of tea-leaves and so on, would be fiercely attacked by the cynical Charles. One October evening with All Hallows Eve in the offing, several of the gentleman of the club sat around a blazing fire in the smoking room discussing the eternal subject of life after death, and of ghosts and various supernatural experiences which some of the members claimed to have had, and Charles was soon ridiculing the notion of souls surviving bodily death. A retired magistrate named Richard, who was one of the oldest members of the Liverpool club, had known Charles for many years, and had heard all of his hackneyed old criticisms of the Occult, and so he decided to lay down a challenge to him in front of seven club members present.

'Charles, if you are so convinced that ghosts are all hogwash, I challenge you to put your money where your mouth is!' Richard said to the cynic, pointing the stem of his pipe at him and fixing a most serious stare upon him. 'I dare you to stay in a church all night with a coffined corpse! There! What do you say to that?'

There followed a tumult of subdued voices from the other members who had heard the extraordinary challenge. Some laughed at the dare and others thought it silly or distasteful.

Charles seemed lost for words for a moment, but then he saw all of the eyes of the club members upon him and rushed to a reply. 'Pray, sir, provide the corpse, coffin and church and I assure you that, on my life, I shall not fail to observe, very punctiliously, your commands!'

Richard puffed on his pipe, coughed, sat up straight in his Bergére armchair, and laid down the basic conditions: 'If you can spend a whole night – from eleven o'clock till five the next morning in a church, in the company of a corpse laid out in an open coffin, I will give you a thousand guineas!'

'A thousand guineas – ha! I'd prefer the hand of your daughter Ada in marriage sir!' came the unexpected reply from Charles in his irritating plummy voice.

Richard shook his head. 'A thousand guineas!'

Charles rose from his chair, and stood with his back to the roaring fire, looking through the windows at the fog blanketing Liverpool outside with a smirk on his face. 'You're obviously not that confident sir, for you know I am more than capable of seeing your challenge through!'

'Very well,' Richard suddenly announced his change of mind, and the club members gasped in disbelief. 'If you can stay in a locked church all night long with a corpse, you can have the hand of my daughter in marriage. If you fail this challenge though, Charles, I will have the entire contents of your wine cellar.'

The men shook hands.

On the very night of Halloween, Charles was taken by Richard to a certain Roman Catholic Church that is still extant today in Liverpool. The priest was paid a good sum of money for the alms box, and he allowed Charles to spend the night in the church with a solitary candle. A parishioner who had recently died was laid out in an open coffin in the central aisle, about thirty feet from the altar, and about twenty feet to the right of the pulpit. Charles seemed very uneasy when he saw the corpse, and he carefully cupped his hand around the candle because there was a draught from somewhere making it flicker and sputter.

'Goodnight Charles,' said Richard, and he and the priest walked to the door of the church. As they men walked away, the clouds parted outside and moonbeams from the full lunar orb streamed through the stained-glass windows, flooding the aisles with multicoloured patches of light and peculiar shadows. Charles heard the key in the lock as the priest turned it, and then he could faintly heard the distant footfalls fading away. A hard silence descended on the church for a few moments, and then Charles heard the horse trot away and the hansom cab it pulled after it trundle away into the night, taking Richard to a nice warm bed. Eerie-sounding gales were whining outside, sending clouds scudding across the skull face of the moon, and now the reality of the challenge hit Charles squarely. If he lost his nerve, how could he even get out of this church? He'd have to go into the vestry where the priests robed before the Mass to break a window and make a humiliating escape.

A paranoid thought crossed the mind of the vintner – had Richard arranged for a living man to be put in a coffin? A man who would suddenly spring to life out of that coffin in an effort to effectuate a heart attack? Well, Charles went with his flickering candle to the coffin and had a look at his only companion on this windy Halloween night. He looked as if he was just sleeping, and for an instant, the dead man's eye seemed to flicker...or was it just a trick of the wavering flame of the cheap tallow candle? The corpse lay there, a man of about forty-five, with dark hair salted with grey at the temples. He wore a badly-cut suit of the sort worn by the lower class tradesmen, and a pair of brown polished brogues. His fists were quite large. Charles gingerly took a closer look. The arms were crossed and the massive fists rested on the chest. They were definitely the fists of a boxer. Then Charles moved the candle to the right side of the dead man's head and saw the tell-tale 'cauliflower ear'. This man had been a pugilist. Charles wondered how he had died. Had it been a violent death or had the end come to this fighter in the form of a microbe that could not even be seen? Had it been a tubercular disease, or pneumonia? It was not useful to dwell on the whys and wherefores in this situation. Charles thought how healthy this man looked even in death; he was at least five feet and seven or even nine inches in height, stretched out here, as he had perhaps been stretched out on the canvas many times during his pugilistic career, until he had squared up to the ultimate opponent who challenges us all in the end – the Grim Reaper. More morbid thoughts came through the mind of the wine-merchant in a chilling stream of consciousness as the moonlight fell in rainbow colours through the church windows onto the long rows of pews and the aisles. How could something as burly and thickset as this man be reduced to mere bones and sludge by the vanquisher worm and the black shiny beetles that begin to 'notice' decomposing flesh through even the wooden shell of the coffin? Other ghastly thoughts swum in the over-active mind of Charles; could the brain of a dead man somehow retain some weak form of consciousness but be unable to signal this continuation of mental activity? This would surely be a form of Hell – to lay rotting in a coffin, feeling every hungry beetle biting into mouldy putrefying flesh with its hungry mandibles; to feel every slithering movement of the worm as it slides through brain and eye-socket...

Enough! Charles went to the altar, and for a moment he seriously considered kneeling and praying, but he was an atheist. He believed that the people of the churches were refugees, taking sanctuary from the harsh findings of scientists. At least that was what Charles said in the safe noon-day world of daylight, with the company of friends around him.

What was that? A shadow of a figure moved out the corner of Charles's eye. As the wine-merchant moved along, his candle had thrown a scrolling shadow from the statue of Jesus. Merely that and nothing more. That banshee wind was screeching now, and when it rattled the heavy oaken door of the church, Charles hoped, in a moment of gleeful optimism that Richard and the priest had returned to cancel the wager, but the door just continued to shake in its frame.

Charles thought of the beautiful Ada's porcelain complexion and her curvaceous body to distract his thoughts from the grim setting, and in his mind he imagined how she would look naked on his bed. He imagined carnal delights and perversions he had never conjured in his lusting mind before, but then he was brought rudely out of his salacious wet daydreams when the candle flame almost set fire to his coat sleeve. Out of reflex action, Charles quickly withdrew his smouldering sleeve from the candle and the current of rapidly displaced air served to extinguish the candle flame. He had lost his only reliable source of light now, and at that moment when the candle was inadvertently snuffed out, the moon slid behind thick opaque clouds.

The church was now almost as dark as the interior of a tomb. Not a single lamp on the street outside could throw even the most feeble light from its gas jet into the church. The dying orange spark on the smouldering candle was blown upon by Charles but it was no use. He was now in the dark. He swore out loud and walked into a bench, injuring his shin. He thought of hurling the damned candle at the altar, but felt even too afraid to let go of it, as if there was some remote chance of it somehow providing light again.

And then the moon broke through the clouds, and Charles hurried over to one of the windows. He was so glad to see that the moon was now set in a fairly wide-open stretch of sky uncluttered with clouds. Charles then had an idea. He thought it might be better if he could sleep in a confession box. He knew deep down he'd feel safer in a confessional, but would not fully admit to this, as he wanted to be a disbeliever. He expected the confession boxes to be locked, but was pleasantly surprised when he turned the brass handle to one, because the door opened. He went inside, closed the door and sat up in the corner. He folded his arms and placed each hand under an armpit in a bid to stay warm. He tried to sleep, but the face of that boxer in the coffin kept putting in an appearance in his mind's eye.

The door of the confession box thumped hard, and Charles opened his eyes with a start. It had to have been the draught from that accursed gale outside. He got up, opened the door and looked into the moonlit church. He could see the upturned face of the corpse. in the coffin from here. Then he noticed something quite peculiar. The bier – the rickety stand the coffin was resting upon, was no longer parallel to the ends of the benches. It looked as if it had moved to the right a few inches. Charles wondered if he had blundered into the stand in the dark when the candle went out. That had to be the reason why the bier looked as if it had moved. It proved useless trying to sleep in the confession box, because the floor was so hard to the vintner's posterior, and so he went to the bench at the back of the church and tried to sleep there. He lay on the bench on his back, and closed his eyes. Once again he thought of Ada, and how, if he could try and sit out this ridiculous wager, he would be able to marry that Venus. He began to drift off when suddenly, he was roused by a noise in the church – it was the screech of something wooden being dragged across the hard tiles of the aisle – like the legs of the coffin stand being ground against the floor! There was a crash, and it echoed back and forth across the cavernous interior of the church. Charles sat bolt upright, and saw that the coffin had overturned! It had fallen from its stand, and the body it had held was lying on the floor.

That body got up off the floor with no difficulty, but walked unsteadily down the aisle – towards Charles, and it groaned and moaned and shouted insensible words. One half of the wine-merchant's mind told him to run into the vestry but the other, more rational side of Charles's mind told him to confront a man who had obviously been hired by

Richard in a ham-fisted attempt to scare him to death. Charles picked up a 5-foot-tall wrought-iron candle-stand and advanced towards the 'resurrected' boxer.

'Drop the ruse man!' he found himself shouting at the staggering figure in the moonlight.

The apparently revived man suddenly adopted a professional stance as if he were squaring up to an opponent in the ring, and when Charles came up close to the man, he placed the candle-stand on the floor of the aisle and smirked at what he perceived as such amateur dramatics. 'How much did he pay you to carry out this scheme, eh?' Charles asked.

The man charged at him and threw a powerful left upper-cut, followed rapidly by a series of jabs from those hammer fists to the vintner's abdomen. Charles fell on his back clutching his broken jaw, unable to breathe because he'd had the wind knocked out of him. He saw the curved ceiling beams of the church go out of focus. And then he lost consciousness.

He awoke in hospital with Richard and several members of the club by his side. Charles tried to speak but his mouth refused to open, because his broken jaw had been wired shut. He swum in and out of consciousness because of the opiates he had been given to kill the pain. He had to communicate with Richard by scrawling words on paper with a pencil, and when he was well enough, Charles accused Richard of setting the whole thing up; of hiring that brute of a boxer – who would now be sued for the vicious assault.

But Richard eventually convinced him that the

truth was much more bizarre. The man in the coffin – a pugilist – had died from alcoholic poisoning – or so the doctor had opined, and no autopsy had been carried out for reasons that were still being investigated. The boxer was dressed and placed in a coffin for a wake at the church, and through some process still unknown to medical science, the "dead man" had regained consciousness for a while. He had probably being disoriented and frightened at finding himself in a coffin in a church in the dead of night with a man who seemed to be challenging him with a big wrought-iron candle-stand. The boxer did what came natural in such a circumstance, and lashed out at a man who would strike him as some sinister figure – and perhaps he even believed he was confronting a thief, for who would have a valid reason for being in a moonlit church that time in the morning?

Anyhow, the poor boxer had been found at the door of the church, quite dead on the floor, close to the font. His heart had given out, and now he had been committed to the earth in a pauper's grave. Richard then informed Charles that the wager had been rendered null and void by the bizarre outcome, and while he would not now be wed to Ada, he would at least retain his wine cellar. After that spine-chilling night spent alone with a dead man, Charles never again voiced his scorn of the supernatural.

THERE'S ALWAYS SOMEONE WATCHING

Many years ago when I was at school, the headmaster – a Mr MacDonald - would come into the assembly hall each morning around nine and deliver some cautionary tale or long-winded parable to the gathering of giggling classes. One particular parable of Mr MacDonald stuck in my mind for some reason, and that was his assertion that there was always someone watching you, and he gave several examples of naughty boys – and men – who had carried out some criminal activity believing that there were no witnesses about, only to subsequently discover that someone had been in the vicinity of the crime watching their every move. The headmaster regaled us with gruesome and seedy tales of murderers who had imagined they had got away with the ultimate crime. He told one tale about a man who had strangled a woman in her bed somewhere off Edge Lane in the 1930s. The killer was unaware that the strangled woman's seven-year-old son had been playing hide and seek just before the murder took place, and had hidden under his mum's bed. As soon as the strangler sneaked out into the evening, the boy tried – unsuccessfully – to revive his mother, then ran helter-skelter to the neighbours, who in turn alerted the police. The strangler was caught within the hour and had been a former neighbour of his victim. After relating more of these morbid little gems to us schoolchildren, the headmaster recapped upon the theme of the assembly discussion - 'So, whenever you're thinking of having a sly smoke in the toilets or stealing something from this school, or, if you are planning to smash one of the windows in the gymnasium and think no one will see you hiding in the alleyway at the back of the school with your catapult, remember this: someone will always be watching you. There's *always* someone watching.'

And today it seems that there really is always someone watching, because we have a record number of closed-circuit television cameras in supermarkets and most shops, and even on buses. If you ride a Hackney cab you'll often see a webcam pointing at you, and of course, there are traffic cameras everywhere. If you are withdrawing money from a hole-in-the-wall ATM machine you'll see a camera mounted on the wall above you inside of a smoked-glass dome, and although there are a staggering two million CCTV cameras in the UK, the crime rate is still soaring, so it would seem that the omnipresent surveillance technology is not acting as a deterrent. Back in 1977, the year the following true story is set in, widescale CCTV was virtually unheard of except in banks, but someone very sinister was watching a certain couple and photographing them in their most intimate moments, and to this day the reasons behind the mysterious surveillance and the methods employed to violate the privacy of the couple remain a mystery.

It all began one sunny afternoon in the August of 1977, on Woodlands Road, Aigburth. A telephone engineer was repairing wires up a telegraph pole near to the old Kelton House of Providence convent when he espied a rather elegant woman walking past down below with her dog. The engineer was a 47-year-old man named Rod and the woman who had caught his eye was 36-year-old Juliet, who lived at a large house on nearby Mossley Hill Road. Rod was single but Juliet was a married woman. On the second occasion that day when Rod saw Juliet walking down the street (on her way to a friend's house), he quickly descended the telegraph pole and said hello to her. Juliet pleasantly said "Hi" back to Rod and walked on, and Rod called after her, 'Excuse me.'

Juliet halted and turned to see what he wanted.

He mopped the sweat from his brow with the back of his hand and said: 'I know this is probably inappropriate of me, but can I just say that I think you're probably the most beautiful girl I've ever seen?'

Juliet seemed lost for words for a moment, and from a distance of about twelve feet away, Rod could see her blush. 'Thankyou,' she replied, and then walked on a few feet, slowed down and turned back to the GPO telephone-repair man. 'I liked the bit about me being a girl,' Juliet quipped, 'haven't been called one of those in a long time.'

And she walked on to her friend's house.

The job could have been wrapped up then and there but Rod decided to continue it on the following day, hoping to see the lovely lady again – and this occurred on the following morning at eleven. Juliet was once again going to her friend Dawn's house, when she saw the telephone engineer ogling her as he knelt in front of an open telephone junction box. She was dressed in a smart topaz-coloured coat and a black knee-length skirt. Rod had to ask her out.

'Morning,' he said to Juliet.

She stopped and said, 'Morning. Working hard are you?' And she looked into the junction box at the multicoloured spaghetti cables and shook her head gently. 'That looks very complicated,' she remarked, and was about to walk on when Rod said: 'My name's Rod by the way.'

'Oh, like Rod Stewart?' Juliet asked with a smile.

'Yeah only I'm not Scottish,' Rod told her, then stood up and asked her outright: 'I'd love to take you for a drink, or better still, for a meal somewhere nice.'

'Rod Stewart isn't Scottish, and my name's Juliet, and erm, I'm married,' came the reply.

'Well? How about it?' Rod persisted, tapping his index finger with a screwdriver.

'I'm married!' Juliet chuckled. She could not believe the audacity of this man, but there was some endearing quality about him she found amusing.

'Well we could have a Platonic meal together

then,' Rod proposed with a deadpan face.

'Oh don't be daft,' Juliet replied and she turned and walked on to her friend's house, and for the remainder of that day she thought about Rod, and almost burned her husband's tea that evening as she kept turning over the compliments Rod had made in her mind.

Juliet's husband Terry was a rather cold fish, and he didn't notice Juliet's far away look. He didn't notice the way she kept walking the dog along Woodlands Road twice a day.

Then, about a week after Rod had first set eyes on Juliet, he was in the city centre one sparkling warm sunny morning, looking at wallpaper patterns at a shop on Bold Street called Willeys, and next door, at that very minute, was Juliet, looking at the shoes in Timpson's. They met as they both left these shops, literally bumping into one another.

'Hello there Juliet!' Rod said, and he looked much smarter now than he had been in those overalls and jeans he had worn on the repair job. Juliet looked a picture of beauty in the eyes of Rod, and she said, 'Oh, hi. Not working today?'

'No, I'm off. It's a beautiful day isn't it?' Rod said, inhaling the fresh morning air as he drew back his broad shoulders.

'Yes, lovely,' Juliet agreed, and then seemed stuck for words. She knew she should just walk on, but she hesitated.

'Let's go for a cup of tea or something,' Rod suggested, and then he asked Juliet: 'Have you had your breakfast?'

'Oh Rod, you're a case,' Juliet shook her head of

long silken hair with a bright smile.

'Come on, we'll have a Platonic breakfast,' he said and he walked to a nearby café with Juliet, and they sat and talked about the places where they were in their lives. Rod's routine was boringly circular without any deviation: he got up, went to work, came home, went the pub, then a curry at the chippy, and back home to bed. Juliet wasn't satisfied with her life; her husband Terry rarely looked directly at her nowadays, and the only affection she received was from her dog Maxwell. She'd tried for years to have children but had been unsuccessful, and suspected it was Terry's fault. She suggested that he and her should go for a fertility test but he said he could happily live without the concern of kids. Juliet also wanted to work but Terry wasn't happy with that either and said he was bringing enough money home from his job as a solicitor.

Well, things went swimmingly that day, and the couple went to St John's Precinct to window shop then parted ways about 3pm, but not before they had arranged a rendezvous for Sunday, which was in two days' time. Juliet told Terry she was going to meet an old schoolfriend in Woolton, and that Sunday morning she rode a hackney cab from her house but a few minutes into the journey she told the cabby to go to another destination instead: Calderstones Park, and there at the gates of the park, she found Rod waiting in his old green Sunbeam Rapier two-door sports saloon.

And they were off to North Wales for the day. After a trip to the Great Orme and a visit to a fairground, the couple booked into a little hotel near

Rhyl as Mr and Mrs Jones, and after a few drinks they made passionate love. Juliet didn't want to go home, and decided to call Terry to tell him she was staying over with her old school chum. 'Yeah, okay,' he had replied in his usual blasé voice, sounding even more coldly dispassionate over the telephone.

That night, Rod and Juliet held on to one another tightly in bed, but around three in the morning, Juliet found herself half awake, and she had the vague impression of someone standing by the bed. 'Is that you?' she murmured, thinking it was Rod, but then she could hear Rod breathing beside her as he slept. Juliet lifted her fatigued head from the pillow and looked around the room. There was no one there. She decided she'd dreamt the bedside visitor.

On the following day at four in the afternoon, Rod dropped Juliet off on Aigburth Road, and she walked home from there. Terry normally didn't get home till after five but he was in the garden with a pair of shears, tidying the hedge. He said 'Hi,' without even looking at his wife, and Juliet went into the house. She saw she had some mail which Terry had put on top of the electricity meter cupboard in the vestibule area, and so she collected the envelopes then went into the lounge, where she saw something which shocked her to the marrow. A large manila envelope lay on the smoked-glass coffee table, and protruding from it were three eight by ten monochrome photographs, and out of curiosity, Juliet pulled them out of the envelope to take a look. They were three photographs of her, lying in bed next to Rod at that hotel. The first thought that crossed Juliet's mind was that Terry had hired a private detective to take the pictures as evidence in some forthcoming divorce case. Juliet picked up the photographs and went into the backyard, ready to leave the house to go to her friend Dawn, but then she realised it was better to have it out with her husband rather than flee the scene. Maxwell came running over to her from his kennel and he whined and tried to jump into her arms, so excited at seeing Juliet again. Terry never bothered taking the dog on its walks or even patted its head.

Juliet made a quick fuss of the dog, then left him in the backyard and went back into the house, down the hallway and out into the garden, where Terry was snipping away. He turned, looked at the photographs his wife was holding, then turned to look back at the hedge he was trimming. 'How long have you been seeing him?' he asked, nonchalantly.

'That was the first day I had spent with him,' Juliet replied, with a numbness in her throat. Her tongue was as dry as sandpaper. 'Did you get someone to take those pictures?'

'No, they just arrived this morning – hand delivered by the looks of it,' Terry told her frostily.

'I don't believe you,' Juliet glared at him. 'I think you hired some snooper, some private detective –'

Terry turned to face her and gritted his teeth. He threw down the shears and they impaled the lawn with their pointed blades. 'I don't give a damn about who you are seeing or what you do! I wouldn't pay good money to have some detective follow someone I couldn't give two hoots about!'

'Is this it, then?' Juliet said to the back of her husband's head as he stormed into the house with the shears still impaled in the lawn.

'Is this what?' he asked, stepping into the hallway.

'Divorce,' Juliet could barely get the word out of her choked-up throat. She wasn't sad over the possible loss of her husband but she was already concerned about Maxwell; would she get custody of the dog?

'I don't know,' Terry turned off the hallway into the kitchen and went to fill the kettle for a cuppa. 'Weren't you happy with me?' he turned to face her at last.

'You're cold,' Juliet grabbed a roll of paper towel, pulled a piece off and dabbed her flooding eyes. 'You never hold me or kiss me – it's not normal Terry. You drove me into his arms.'

'You obviously have some enemies,' he said with a meditative expression as he gazed out the window into the backyard.

'What do you mean?' Juliet was baffled by the remark.

'Well who took those pictures of you and - him? Or were you with another man as well? Did he take them?'

Juliet grimaced at the warped imaginings of her emotionally detached husband. 'No, I wasn't with two men, Rod's enough – more than any man I could hope for.'

This statement didn't even affect Terry; he didn't even wince at Juliet's damning words.

'Someone took those photographs, and they went

to a lot of trouble to drop you in it,' Terry reflected, then turned to make eye contact. 'I give you my word, I did not hire a private detective. Now, if you want to call it a day, just let me know and we can go about this like civilized people.'

He put the kettle on and got his usual cup from the hook.

Juliet went into the backyard and sat playing with Maxwell, but a tear dripped onto the dog's snout and it sensed Juliet was upset, and it whined and jumped on her knee and licked her face.

She decided she wanted to give Terry another chance, and he promised her he'd be more attentive and for the first few weeks he took her out to some expensive restaurants and took her to see a few plays, as Juliet enjoyed the theatre, but he soon went back to his old cold ways, and by October, Juliet was longing for Rod again. One evening as she walked Maxwell, Juliet went into a telephone box and called Rod, but he seemed distant and so different. 'Is someone there with you?' she asked him, and after a pause, he said, 'Yes, I'll get back to you on that wiring job Stan. Give me a ring on Wednesday.' And then he hung up.

On Wednesday, Juliet intended to ring Rod, but felt cheap. She went into the callbox but decided not to go ahead with all this cloak and dagger stuff anymore. She left the telephone box and walked Maxwell home.

On the following morning at nine, there was a knock at the door of Juliet's home. She thought it was the postman delivering a package for her husband (who had left for work thirty minutes before), but when she answered, she saw Rod standing on the doorstep. 'What are you doing coming here?' she asked, and she looked beyond him at the house facing where an elderly neighbour was usually to be seen at her net curtains.

'You didn't call,' Rod said, one hand in his pocket. He looked bothered, and his face was lanced with disappointment.

'Come in!' Juliet stepped aside and when Rod passed her on his way down the hall, she took a few furtive looks left and right, just in case someone was watching – and she was especially mindful of those photographs.

Juliet closed the door, and when she went into the living room, she saw Rod sitting on the sofa with Maxwell at his feet. The dog was on its back, and Rod was tickling his tum.

'What's his name?' Rod asked, smiling at the contented animal.

'Are you seeing someone else now?' Juliet wanted to know, and she sat in Terry's armchair, about six feet away from Rod and studied his facial expression very carefully indeed as he replied.

'No,' was his simple answer, and he stroked Maxwell's head, then looked back at Juliet's sceptical face. 'No! What makes you think I'm seeing someone, hey?' Rod's nostrils flared at the half-accusation.

'The way you spoke to me when I called you,' Juliet told him frankly, 'that's what made me think you were with someone. Calling me Stan?'

'My brother was visiting, that's all – '

'So why wouldn't you want him to know you were

seeing someone? Come on Rod – '

'You don't know what Harry's like. He's a born-again Christian for a start and if he knew I was seeing a married woman he'd have me exorcised; he's a real Bible-basher. The less he knows the better; our business would be all over the parish,' Rod explained, and seemed quite ruffled at Juliet's scepticism.

'Hmm, ' Juliet muttered, and she went to the sideboard and took out the manila envelope with the three incriminating photographs. She laid them out on the coffee table, and for the first time she heard Rod swear.

'What's this?' he asked, horrified and somewhat perplexed.

Juliet pushed one of the photographs toward Rod. 'Someone took pictures of us at that hotel near Rhyl, obviously while we were asleep. I thought my husband was behind it at first, but he wasn't. So who took them?'

'It's *got* to be him, he must have known you were going to sleep with me…'

Juliet shook her head. 'Terry's many things but he isn't a liar. I just know he wasn't behind this. It's very strange. I don't know how anyone would have had access to the bedroom – besides the hotel staff of course, but what would they get out of this and how would they know my address?'

'It doesn't make sense.' Rod picked up one of the photographs and studied it close.

'The funny thing is that I only remembered something earlier on which might have some bearing on this,' Juliet told her lover. 'That night at the hotel, I remember being sort of half awake and half asleep, and I thought I saw someone standing over me in the bed, but I dismissed it as a dream and went back to sleep.'

Rod thinned his eyes and then went into a brown study. 'Do you remember that old man in the bar of the pub? He had an Irish accent; he was quite small and he said we made a fine couple?'

'Yes; yes I do, he said he was from Tipperary,' Juliet recalled. 'You don't think it's him?'

Rod shrugged. 'I'm probably clutching at straws, but you never know. Perhaps he knows your husband – '

'I had never met that man before that evening, and I'm sure I would have recognised any friends of Terry,' Juliet said, pouring cold water on Rod's theory.

'Well someone took these pictures. It's a real mystery,' said Rod, putting the pictures down on the coffee table. 'Can I show them to a friend named Alec? He's an expert on photography and he might be able to tell us a few things.'

'No!' Juliet picked up the photographs and put them in the manila envelope, 'Let's just forget it all. Probably just some weirdo – a Peeping Tom out to cause trouble.'

Well, Rod kissed Juliet and wanted to take it further but Juliet was adamant that there would be no sex in her house. She arranged to meet Rod in a few days at a café on Lark Lane.

On the following morning at 7.55am, Rod got out of bed, and his girlfriend Nancy tried to prevent him from going downstairs to pick up the mail that the postman had just delivered. 'Come here you,' she said, and she tried to pull his Y-fronts off but he intercepted her hand and laughingly told her to get up. He had to be in work for eight-thirty. He went downstairs and picked up the bundle of usual junk mail, gas bills and a few other envelopes – including a rather large thin manila one. It had no address written on it. As Rod looked at it, Nancy appeared behind him and asked if he would like bacon, eggs and sausages. Rod nodded, and went cold, for he realised that the big brown envelope looked just like the one Juliet had showed him; the one that had contained the three photographs.

'Bills eh?' Nancy said, and she meant to take them off Rod but he pulled them away and his face had undergone a terrible change. Before he had looked sleepy and easygoing but now he looked like a man possessed. Nancy was merely going to tell him to put
all the bills away until after breakfast, but now she sensed there was something he didn't want her to see among those envelopes, and she asked him what it was. 'What's in that envelope?'

'Nothing, just nothing okay?' came the nervous reply.

'Let me see then,' Nancy asked, and now her suspicion was at fever pitch. What the hell was Rod hiding?

'It's private business, okay?' Rod told her and hurried out of the hallway to the toilet.

Nancy swore as he went and said, 'Make your own breakfast!'

In the toilet, Rod opened the large manila

envelope and recoiled in shock at the three pictures. Three monochrome photographs – all eight by ten prints – of him kissing Juliet at her home yesterday morning. How had the photographer obtained these shots? Rod calculated - from what he could remember of the layout of Juliet's living room – that only someone with a telephoto lens would be able to take those pictures from a point that lay somewhere elevated on Woodlands Road, not far from the convent, but the idea of a snooping nun was quickly dismissed of course. This vindictive snapper had to be someone local who had taken the shots from the window of his - or her - house on Woodlands Road. Rod hid the photographs under a mat in the toilet then put some of the junk mail into the eight by ten inch manila envelope. He pulled the chain, left the toilet and apologised to Nancy for snapping at her earlier, but the 22-year-old was getting dressed.

'All that envelope contained was junk mail,' Rod told the sulking young redhead, but Nancy ignored him, and went into the toilet. A few minutes later she emerged holding the photographs. She'd somehow found them under the mat, or perhaps she had known he'd hid something from that envelope in the toilet. 'She's old as well,' Nancy said, eyeing the picture of Rod and Juliet in a passionate embrace. 'Ah, well, never mind, Rod, you need a woman nearer your age.'

'It's an old photograph!' he said, lamely.

'No it's not, you've got your new jacket on in that stupid picture,' Nancy pointed out.

And she left that morning in tears.

Rod telephoned Juliet and as soon as he heard the receiver being lifted he said, 'You're not going to believe this!'

'Hello? Who is this?' said Terry. Juliet's husband had taken the morning off for a dental appointment.

'Oh, sorry, I've dialled the wrong number,' Rod cringed and firmly put the receiver down. He took the photographs to his friend Alec, a photographic expert, and asked him if he could deduce anything about the mystery photographer.

'Ilford photographic paper. Available from most photographic suppliers. I get mine from Samson Cameras on Bold Street,' said Alec, scrutinising the faint brand name watermarked across the back of the three snaps. 'I'd say he used fast film, about 400 ASA maybe, and from the depth of field, a good telephoto lens. Must have used a tripod to keep it that steady...' And he waffled on about the mysterious photographer using technical terms that meant nothing to Rod.

'Do you think he's a professional photographer?' Rod asked.

'He's good, but he might just be a good amateur, its hard to say. Who's the lovely lady anyway?' Alec asked with an admiring eye on Juliet.

'Just a friend,' Rod told him with a sigh.

On the following morning, Rod parked a hundred yards from Juliet's home, and he watched as her husband drove off to work at eight-thirty. Rod then drove round the neighbourhood for about ten minutes, then called on Juliet again. She was furious at him calling yet again at the house, but he showed her the photographs of himself and her kissing as they embraced. 'Came this morning, probably before the postman arrived, as there's no franking mark or any address on the envelope.'

Juliet stood there looking at one of the photographs with her hand over her mouth. She seemed very shocked. 'Who's doing this?' she asked, and looked towards the windows feeling ever so paranoid.

Rod followed the line of her gaze and he stood looking directly through the window above the nets. There was a house across the street where that photograph must have been taken from. The curtains to the bedroom where the snooper must have taken the picture were drawn. 'It's got to have been taken from that window,' Rod told Nancy, and she cast a very nervous glance at the window in question.

'I'm going to get to the bottom of this once and for all,' Rod announced, and he suddenly walked towards the hallway, his arms swinging to and fro like pistons.

Juliet flew after him. 'No! Don't Rod! There's an old woman who lives in that house and she's the biggest gossip in the street! Don't go! She'll tell Terry!'

'I won't have people taking liberties with me!' snarled Rod, and he pushed Juliet out the way as she tried to stand in front of him. He left the house and marched across the street. Juliet stood in her hallway, watching him approach the door of the nosy old neighbour.

Rod hammered on the knocker, and almost half a

minute past before the door opened and a woman in her seventies with a hearing aid asked him if he could read.

'What are you talking about?' said Rod.

The old woman pointed to the brass sign on her door which said: 'No Hawkers or Unsolicited Mail".

'I'm not selling anything,' Rod told the elderly woman, 'Is there a person in your house who's in the habit of taking pictures of people in their homes?'

'What are you talking about?' the aged woman trembled at Rod's raised voice.

'You'll be getting a letter from my solicitor if this doesn't stop!' he promised, then walked back to Juliet's house.

Enough was enough. Juliet told Rod if he did something stupid like that ever again, she'd end their affair. Rod calmed down and had a coffee. After much contemplation on this unusual predicament, he told Juliet: 'It's got to be that old nosy parker; how else could anyone take a picture from that angle?' And he picked up the photograph and held it up, working out the angle it must have been taken at.

'There's also a telegraph pole over there someone could have taken it from – did you ever think of that?' Juliet told her lover. 'Maybe one of your friends in the GPO could have taken it.'

Rod thought about that for a moment and went cold. 'Nah, not one of the people I work with knows I'm seeing you, so we can discount that one.'

'Are you sure?' Juliet asked with one eyebrow raised.

Rod closed his eyes and nodded. 'I'm certain,' he replied, then opened his eyes and looked at the ceiling, 'but wait a minute, that morning in the café on Bold Street, didn't that waitress say she recognised me as the man who fixed her telephone?'

'Oh this has nothing to do with her, Rod, she was just a waitress. She's not a photographer and how would she know we were going to a hotel in North Wales? And how would she know where I lived? This bastard – whoever it is – is making us paranoid. We're suspecting everyone of being him.'

'Or her,' Rod chipped in, 'let's not be sexist. The weird thing is that someone, somewhere, might even be taking pictures of us right now.'

Juliet went straight to the window and shut the curtains. It was now so dark she had to switch the light on.

She sat on the sofa with Rod, and snuggled against his chest as he stroked her hair. Within minutes they were making love on that sofa.

And on the following day, just before Terry set off for work, Juliet went to the front door with him and to her utter horror, she saw one of those accursed 8 by 10 inch manila envelopes on the doormat. Before Terry noticed it, Juliet shouted: 'Phone!' at the top of her voice. Terry halted just before the vestibule door and gave a puzzled look at his wife. 'I didn't hear the phone,' he said.

'Yes, it's ringing, can't you hear it? It's ringing in your study!' Juliet told him, standing in front of him.

'I must be going deaf,' Terry said, and he went towards his study, which was a room off the hallway, and Juliet picked up the manila envelope, rushed into the lounge, and placed it under a bundle of magazines on the coffee table.

'You're hearing things,' Terry said, returning to the hallway. 'The phone wasn't ringing, you must have tinnitus. See you later.'

And he left the house and got into his trusty old Morris Oxford. As soon as he had driven out of sight, Juliet took a sharp intake of breath and opened the manila envelope, guessing correctly what it contained – three of those black and white photographs – and these ones were very graphic, for they showed Juliet and Rod in the throes of sexual intercourse on the sofa. Someone, somewhere out there has the negatives to these pictures, Juliet thought as she shuddered. This time the photograph had been taken at an angle which suggested that the photographer had been standing in her lounge, which was, of course, impossible – and yet the curtains had been drawn, so how else would anyone be able to take a picture? This eerie aspect – the plain impossibility of taking a photograph in such circumstances – really creeped out Juliet. She later showed the photographs to Rod, then burned them in the garden one morning after Terry had gone to work. Juliet then decided she had to stop seeing Rod; the affair had to end, for she felt that the unknown photographer was some perverted moralist who was trying to tell her to refrain from any sexual activity outside of her marriage. Rod begged her to stay with him, but Juliet said she didn't want to see him again. It was hard to stay away from Rod, even after she eventually found out (from a friend) about Nancy, the young student he had been having an affair with, but as soon as Juliet stopped seeing Rod, no more of those large manila envelopes arrived.

Juliet was 71 when she told me about the strange affair of the enigmatic photographer, and she had had many years to ponder the mystery. What did she make of it? She remained as baffled today as she had been when she was in her mid-thirties, all those years ago. I asked her if she had come to suspect anyone of being the secret snapper over the years, and she recalled how, a few years after the strange incidents, she was at a friend's birthday party in Chester, when a tall thin man of about fifty, with a very pallid complexion and large dark brown eyes came up to her. This man, known only as Dean to a few of those who remembered him, remarked to Juliet: 'You're very photogenic. You don't remember me do you? I took photographs of you when you graduated at university. You're one subject I never forgot.'

This set alarm bells off in Juliet's mind. She could just remember her graduation and vaguely recalled getting her photograph taken in a certain Liverpool studio in the city centre. Dean asked to be excused, and said he was going the toilet, but never returned, and when Juliet asked several of the people at the party if they knew Dean's surname, none could recall it. Then, about a week after the party, a manila envelope arrived at Juliet's home, and it was the exact same dimensions as those ones which caused so much consternation back in 1977. Inside, there was a single black and white print of Juliet at the party in Chester. Juliet – and no other guest at the party – could recall anyone carrying a camera, except the cheap instamatic one the boyfriend of the girl who was celebrating her birthday had used, whereas the picture of Juliet had obviously been taken with what seems to have been a single-lens reflex (SLR) camera. There were no messages or notes in the manila envelope, just the 8 by 10 photograph, and the envelope bore a Manchester postmark. This does not mean of course, that "Dean" was the eerie photographer who seemed bent on exposing cheats, but Juliet feels that strange tall man was trying to tell her something when he told her she was *photogenic.*

Printed in Great Britain
by Amazon